Gratitude for Soul in the Driver's Seat

"As a long-time student and lover of the original *A Course in Miracles*, I was totally stumped trying to share its wisdom with my six children, aged 18 to 24, as they came to me with their fears and struggles. Along comes *Soul in the Driver's Seat: A Course in Miracles for Today*! Now I am able to point them to simple and relevant *Soul* truths which right away hit home with them. What peace for me! What a gift!"

—Rak Dixit, Enterprise Architect

"*Soul* is showing me my true purpose in life. As I reflect on the daily lessons my moments of inner peace and love are growing. I experience far less fear about our chaotic world, and my 30-year marriage is healthier than it has ever been!"

—Joanie Dezember

"It's as if Jesus is saying, "Can you hear me now? The ego's gotta go!" The daily no-nonsense questions in this new *A Course in Miracles*, expose the ego once and for all. With soul firmly back in the driver's seat, the truth dawns on us—the emperor (the ego) has no clothes! And our fears evaporate."

—Rev. Helen Burke, Author of *Just Tell Them I Love Them*

"The daily readings of *Soul* are short and to the point. This helps both of us to settle in, be truly present with their meaning, and carry them into the work of our day. It is a lovely way to begin each morning together."

—Leland and Tegan Wong-Daugherty, Teachers & Land Stewards, Canada

"*Soul* takes the reader right to the heart of *A Course in Miracles*. It is a simple yet profound guide to life's most persistent questions, offering a direct way to an authentic life, rich with love and free from ego fear."

—Rodrigo Cayres, Co-Publisher, Take Heart Publications

"This delightful new book is filled with life-changing truths written with such clarity and simplicity! I use it daily for myself, and often with my clients to whom it offers comfort, emotional relief, and inspiration to live more fully and freely. Enjoy!"

—Dr. Timothy O'Higgins, Clinical Psychologist

"Want to know the difference between what you were told you are and the truth of what you actually are? *Soul*'s daily insights are brief and simple. Nothing airy-fairy. Just the truth. Soul food. Feed yourself daily."

—Jude Junghans, Group Facilitator

"The messages of *Soul* are extremely helpful to me. They accompany me in every minute and their effect grows stronger in me each day. I need them! We all need them!"

—Jacques Tétrault, Canada

"*Soul* has been transformative for me. Its questions and insights, offered in simple conversational language, help me live each moment with greater clarity, meaning, connection, acceptance, and authenticity."

—Migdalia Wills, Divine Design Coaching

"I absolutely love everything about *Soul* — the guidance, the easy-to-read format, and the daily reflections. Words fail to describe how precious it is to me! I feel so connected to Jesus and to all around me in each holy instant, and I know I will never lose my way again."

—Cynthia Pitt

"As a lifelong seeker I have read, practiced, and meditated at length. Yet *Soul*'s incisive questions now propel me into a whole new place of unconditional love and the freedom of knowing who I truly am."

– Lorraine Desroches, Retired Chaplain, Canada

"A must read for every person who wishes to understand what is happening now on Mother Earth, at both the physical and spiritual levels. It is written in plain, simple English. As you read, you will feel peace and harmony grow within you, regardless of the chaos in the outside world."

—Paul Gobeil, Canada

"*Soul in the Driver's Seat* is truly heart-expanding. The inner voice of my soul is now louder, clearer, and much easier to follow."

—Gail Rogers

"*Soul* is a key that opened a locked door. Curiosity urged me to step inside. I did. And I found a way to my heart where I now rest in the realization that I have never been lost."

—Jodi Donohue, Australia

"*Soul* has given me a fresh perspective on life's complex problems and it offers solutions! I am coming to live life fully knowing that I am loved unconditionally."

—Judith Leykauf, Canada

"I am truly enjoying these precious messages. The truth they offer—that we are divine souls—is so encouraging!"

—Lode Langeweg, The Netherlands

"*Soul* offers a new understanding of familiar topics, along with daily reflections that deepen my awareness and practice of living in unconditional love. Joining with others we discover and celebrate our Oneness."

—Rev. Bill Heller

SOUL

IN THE DRIVER'S SEAT

A COURSE IN MIRACLES FOR TODAY

RECEIVED BY
RICHARD CURTIS GREATHOUSE

Richard Curtis Greathouse
Soul in the Driver's Seat: A Course in Miracles for Today

CoCreating Clarity
Copyright © 2025 by Richard Curtis Greathouse
First Edition

Softcover ISBN 979-8-9998729-0-6
eBook ISBN 979-8-9998729-1-3

Cover Design | Amanda Jo Nagle
Interior Design | Ashley Russell Designs
Editor | Lee Reznicek Editing
Dedication Illustration | Amanda Jo Nagle

Dedicated to YOU the reader. Your courageous choice to dive wholeheartedly into this book will transform your life and change the world.

Originating in central Asia, the tulip was cultivated in the Ottoman Empire as early as the fourteenth century, where it was a symbol of royalty, perfection, and paradise on earth. *Soul in the Driver's Seat* offers a path to *"where heaven and earth are one state."* And the tulip is the perfect symbol for all this means – unconditional love, freedom, and the grandeur of divine power.

It is one thing to know you have a soul, but it is another one entirely to know that you are one.
(V1:8.1.2)

We want to promote peace and love with less ego, less fear, more soul, and more love. This may sound impossible in today's crazy world, but this is the only hope here.
(V1:7.6.4)

The soul's purpose is to express unconditional love in a place that is hostile to it. It is this simple, and it is this difficult.
(V3:4.4)

Contents

Volume One

Volume Two

Volume Three

Soul Companion

Prologue

How This Book Came To Be

It was in 2006, while clearing out my brother's room after he died, that I first encountered *A Course in Miracles* (*ACIM*). As I was going through his things, I came across the now-familiar blue book and realized that he'd been studying *ACIM's* deep metaphysical messages of truth! That was a surprise. Holding the book in my hand, I silently heard, *"Do you want to read this?"* I was ill at the time and was about to have major surgery, so my answer was *"No, I'm not ready!"*

Seven years later I was ready. I bought myself a copy of *ACIM* and read it twice, once in 2013 and again in 2014. And that's when I discovered the just-published combined volume of *A Course of Love* (*ACOL*). This beautiful book grabbed my heart and cracked it wide open! I simply could not put it down. I must have read it cover to cover fifteen times or more over the next few years – 2014 to 2020. And that's when I heard that I was going to receive a brand-new book that was a continuation of *ACOL*, and a completion of what began with the original *ACIM* in 1965. It was February 7, 2020, one month before the start of the COVID-19 pandemic lockdown.

And so began almost six years of my receiving and writing. Most of these books are available on the *A Journey into the Unknown* and *Arrival* websites. There are a few that have not been seen by the public and one that even I haven't read. The first three parts of the book you hold in your hand, *Soul in the Driver's Seat: A Course in Miracles for*

Today, were received over a six-month period during the summer and fall of 2022. They were written in segments, as I was called upon at all times of day and night and especially during the early morning hours. I would listen and write, then get myself ready and go off to my full time day job as a Special Education teacher at a high school in the city.

When I was first informed that this brand new *A Course in Miracles* would be written, I literally said, *"Oh, Hell No!"* I'm not kidding either! I knew that the original *ACIM* had taken seven years to receive and write down. And I simply could not imagine fulfilling this request, which honestly felt a lot more like a demand! Yet in the end, I relented, and the initial handwritten manuscript was completed in September 2022. Little did I know then that it was only *Volume One*. When I was informed that there would be two more parts, I was so furious that steam must have been coming out of my ears! Calming myself down I went to Walgreens, selected a second notebook, and by November that year, *Volumes Two* and *Three* were complete.

You're likely wondering – how does all of this work? The answer is I am clairaudient. I can hear unseen beings talking to me. Imagine a manager in a company dictating to her secretary. Well, I'm the secretary, the difference being that I cannot see the manager! All I do is make myself available, listen, receive, and write down what comes, word for word. I don't go through any kind of writing process. I don't brainstorm, draft, or edit. I don't know anything about what I am receiving nor where it is going. I do know how many times a day Jesus wants to meet and the approximate times. Most sessions are between twenty and thirty minutes, and I manage to squeeze them in around my full-time job. Although I have no idea what any session will be about, it all weirdly ends up making sense. And you'll be pleased to know that *Soul in the Driver's Seat* was a lot more fun for me than many of the other books I've received.

In the spring of 2024, I heard another figurative knock on my door. And guess what? There was going to be a fourth part to *Soul in the Driver's Seat* called *Soul Companion*! I knew that *Soul Companion* was going to focus on two years of journal prompts correlating with the two years of daily reflections – *Steps to Authenticity* and *The Gift of Wisdom* – offered in *Volume One*. Although I couldn't quite see how Jesus' accompanying narratives complemented the journal prompts, until Christina suggested a few tweaks to improve clarity and flow. At this point I was completely worn out and ready to hang up my channeling shoes! Yet here I am! Still willingly making myself available more than a year later! And feeling so very grateful to have completed this amazing book – *Soul in the Driver's Seat, A Course in Miracles for Today* – for you and for everyone who discovers its magical and practical wisdom in the years ahead.

Rick Greathouse
Special Education Teacher & Reluctant Receiver
October 2025

Soul in the Driver's Seat
A Course in Miracles for Today

Volume One

Chapter One

Introduction

1. It is I, the one known as Jesus. I penned the original *A Course in Miracles* and now I have returned to create a new and updated version for the times we face. To quote Bob Dylan, "The times they are a-changin'." The original book was quite an undertaking to both write and read for the common man. It was incomprehensible to most but the most ardent, who would spend years attempting to understand it. Now it is my desire to create by recreating and make the content from the original so simple and understandable that it can reach a brand-new audience. There is an honest hunger for truth out there but little to be found. If I can explain the basics, then there is more advanced material available about applying and living a lifestyle of truth as your true self. May this serve as a warning. There is danger ahead. If you proceed in reading this, you may not be able to stop and may be drawn to more channeled texts by me and others. You can say that your soul may find it all refreshingly addictive, so be warned. There may be no turning back, but really, why would you? Your life is just about to begin again as a type of rebirth or awakening to parts of yourself you didn't know existed. Let the process begin.

2. What is a miracle, you may ask? Many things in the world of form are miraculous. Everything from animals to insects to the wide variety of plant life, and everything in between, is miraculous. The human body is miraculous, as are the elements of the earth, wind, and fire. Time

itself is miraculous. Advances in medicine and technology are miraculous. The ability to use a brain to process information and plan a response is miraculous. But what is a miracle?

3. Simply put, a miracle is a change in perception. A miracle is a change from perceived ideas to the possibility that there may be much more going on than the human senses indicate. A miracle is a shift from limitation to expansiveness, from a definition to something that cannot be defined. Miracles are performed by miracle workers, and who might these be? A miracle worker is a human who has had their sixth sense awakened. The sixth sense is a sensitivity or awareness of the unseen aspects of life. Once fully operational, a human with now six senses can use the brain artfully and strategically, in ways that enhance what only five operating senses could do on their own. This is a miracle. It is a great evolutionary step that enables what fuels the body to be reflected in the day-to-day operations of the body.

4. What is it that operates or gives life to a body, whether it is human or nonhuman?

5. Just as it is a hand that operates a puppet or marionette, it is also a hand, so to speak, that operates a body, any type of body. This hand is figurative, but in literal terms it is a very small part of something bigger.

6. This something bigger is what is known as source energy, commonly known as God, and the figurative hand is commonly known as a soul. This soul is your true self. It is highly individualized as there are no two that are alike. The body's operating system, known as ego, tricks you into thinking that you are something you are not.

7. It wants you to believe that you are not a soul, an aspect of the creator of the universe, but instead are a complicated person with likes, dislikes, a history, and a projected future. This is the great con, but who is it who created this great con? It was all souls as totality who decided to take on this great adventure in pretending to be something we are not.

8. Strengthening ourself through adversity of all types is the only way to grow more of it. This "it" that I refer to is source energy. This is God. God is here to grow more of itself, the nature of which is benevolent care and concern for itself in the form of others. God is here to help itself to grow. It grows through relationship each and every time love is chosen over fear.

9. This is the basic foundation for a process that has grown quite complex and is completely hidden from view. Virtually no one knows any of this is going on because virtually everyone is lost in the illusion of being a human, with likes, dislikes, a history, and a projected future. Being human is only a means to an end. It is not what it seems to be. Humans are part of something else and that something else is the divine God energy in themselves and in all. Humans are not really independent contractors as they all think they are.

10. The ego uses a mound of clay (the brain) to do its bidding. Everything revolves around me, myself, and I. It seeks power first and foremost. It evaluates everything and everyone and wants to know their effects on itself. The ego seeks power in order to control and seek out advantages in all aspects of life. While it is allowed to believe it has control, this is part of the illusion of being human. It is allowed to make choices, to either be in alignment with this larger presence I have already alluded to or suffer the consequences. Suffering is and has always been widespread in the human world because the ego is a harsh master.

11. A chair is a chair because it has been given meaning, and this meaning has been passed down through the generations. Human thought is cumulative and progressive. A thought can be supported through time and experience, or rejected and replaced by another thought that is believed to be true as time and circumstances change. The world is no longer thought to be flat, but hot items are still believed not to warrant touch until they cool substantially.

12. Gravity works whether one believes in it or not, but not having sex before marriage was widely believed in at one time and is now widely rejected. Some thoughts and concepts require buy-in. One person may buy into a concept due to fear of eternal damnation in a lake of fire being supervised by demons armed with pitchforks, while others have no such inhibitions.

13. Being human and experiencing the world through the human lens is very much a package deal. Unless someone is on a desert island, an individual human is dependent on many others for food, clothing, housing, transportation, education, and care until they themselves can help do all of this for others.

14. The human experience is an interactive relationship with billions of seemingly separate parts. This is the human illusion because what seems to be isn't what is really transpiring at all. The oneness within the multitude is growing and becoming more aware of itself.

15. The fundamental difference in how the ego and divine oneness see anything is that the soul sees purpose in everything, whereas the ego sees things as a means to an end or as a final product in a process. To the ego, everything revolves around it. Everything either supports the ego or is in opposition to it while simultaneously being in support of other egos. This is how simple objects become status symbols or memory holders or even signs of weakness.

16. Both the ego and the soul have the ability to see something as simple as a chair or a fork, but it is the ego who sees remembrances of itself everywhere it looks. Therefore, the ego does not see clearly. The soul sees clearly because it sees the Divine everywhere it looks. It sees the eternal, timeless, nonchanging quality within the temporary, and everything here is, in fact, temporary. The soul honors itself by admitting that it is here in a world filled with the temporary, whether they are treasured objects, thrown-away junk, or human characters. It is the soul

combined with other souls who created it all, with a singular purpose in mind.

17. Overcoming the power of the ego is the purpose for any world of form and yes, there are many of them, too many to count. It is true that you are not alone on the earth. This is true in more ways than one. Whatever the world's human population is, double it to get an idea of how many character puppets there are, and how many souls there are operating each and every one. The character puppets were all designed to believe they are real and they each do, so to humor them we will double the population. Most character puppets have little to no useful information about their own souls, other than maybe hearing about them in a movie or a song. This is the great illusion. It isn't that objects aren't really present in the environment. It's that character puppets think they are character puppets. They don't know that they are souls operating character puppets, becoming stronger while doing so. Souls are aspects of God and God is something that grows. It grows in strength and power. There are many, many places on the earth and there are many, many situations on the earth, where there just isn't enough God energy to positively affect an otherwise negative situation or climate. Until a character puppet allows its own soul to ask for and receive outside assistance, none is offered. Character puppets think they are in charge and the universe allows them to think this. It is an illusion.

18. Human identity and human thought create an illusionary reality that covers up a true reality. They are merely symptoms meant and designed to be overcome. The overcoming process is known as awakening, a precious beginning of a process when a human discovers their true identity and operates from that understanding. It is the convergence of the eternal with the temporary. Human identity and thought create the illusion that someone is something they are not. Divine identity and thought with the Christ Mind marry the two states of timeless and

timebound, completing the circle of life. When a soul has gained enough maturity to take control from the body's natural operating system, the ego, then Christ has returned. Sanity has replaced irrational and insane thought and actions. This has already started happening across the land one soul at a time. This is the Second Coming of Christ. This is *Soul in the Driver's Seat: A Course in Miracles for Today*. It is a guidebook for those who want to awaken and explore their own true identity, which will culminate in soul growth that will produce Christ, an operating system that reflects God in mankind. Let it be.

19. This is the end of the introduction.

Chapter Two
The Basics

1. The ego doesn't ever see the full picture of anything. It sees parts and then fills in the blanks for the rest. Its opinions and harsh rhetoric about everything add to the mix and you end up with a very distorted image, whether it is of a person or a situation.

2. There has not been an alternative available until now. I showed one example of the alternative during my time on the earth. It was not accurately recorded or understood. No one understood that being Christ had anything to do with them, other than it being something to believe in so that your sins could be washed away and gain favor with God. I became a worshipped deity, not an equal contemporary. I showed a way and now it's your turn. There will be some work involved. I can promise you that much. Changing your body's operating system while it actively fights you for doing so, moment to moment, has not been easy for the select few who have accomplished it in the modern age. It won't be easy for you either, but the rewards will far exceed the hardship. For any effort you invest in this process will be multiplied considerably because what will really transpire will be your own soul rejoining the fold while still in form. This is where all of the extra help will come from.

3. This chapter will be called "The Basics."

4. Love, the unconditional variety, is the only real thing in this world. It is true one hundred percent of the time. It is eternal and timeless. It is complete concern for itself in the form of others. It enhances other

bodies of love or souls who may be in difficult circumstances when their egos will not listen to them and carry out their own loveless agendas instead. Love sees the forms that manifest when there is little love that is powerful enough to counteract them, but respects the process, the very slow, painstakingly slow, process.

5. What is not love is fear, and fear is not in itself real. Fear is simply a call for love, however devastating it may be, however destructive, however much suffering it causes. Fear calls for love and rarely receives it. What fear usually receives is fear. Fear on top of fear is a recipe for disaster, and this explains many things in the world, both the small and the large.

6. The human experiment and experience is basically one of duality. Love from the soul is always seeking to be heard, but fear from the brain drowns it out and prevents it from expressing as often as it would like. When this happens, programming and conditioning typically triumph, and nothing too terribly devastating happens. But on occasion, horrific scenes of both cruelty and destruction on small and mass scales occur, which do nothing but exponentially increase fear.

7. Humans and souls have a very different take on things. Humans will say that so and so is a murderer. Souls will say that so and so is a soul who did everything within its power to stop the character-mind-body vehicle from committing a murder. Souls will say that the recipe for the murder was made long ago when the quasi-real puppet began to bottle up feelings and resentments, creating a ticking time bomb known as rage. As souls mature, they have a greater capacity to handle characters with needs such as this.

8. Fear vs. Love is the first dilemma on the earth. Love is not against fear, but fear is against love for all intents and purposes. The fear factor here is disproportionate to the love factor here, the unconditional, no matter what, love factor. Fear often disguises itself as love. Fear is nice and

kind when it has ulterior motives. This is the best it can do. It does these things to paint a rosy picture of itself as a caring and loving entity. This couldn't be further from the truth because the truth is that the ego is a con artist: a liar in all ways.

9. There are two selves. The outer one is the body, personality, and character. It is considered an illusion because it is temporary. It is fueled by something real, although it itself is not real. It has everyone fooled – both those who are here now and everyone who has ever been here. This illusion of something real, an aspect of God as soul, who is pretending to be something completely contrary to its own nature, is an illusion. An illusion virtually no one can find their way out of while they are here. It's that good of an illusion. It's so convincing that even the strongest souls have a great deal of trouble dealing with it.

10. Who created the illusion? The ego combined with all other egos created the illusion. Who created the ego? The collective of God did. Why? This is the only way that God can grow more of itself. The ego provides fear, which is the resistance that is needed for God to grow. What is God? God is unconditional love, care, and consideration for itself and others. What is an ego? An ego is everything that God is not.

11. You are not the thing that looks back at you in the mirror. This has been your true self's friendly sparring partner at best, and its archenemy at worst. You are an invisible, formless quality that took form many years ago. Before that birth, you died out of another lifetime in form that you were born into and lived. You may have been a janitor who could barely read or sign their name, or you may have been a soldier in a war, or the wife of one who had to bury her husband. In other words, you've been around many, many times, and each time you, the true you, grew a little more. Maybe the growth was infinitesimally small during a particular lifetime or maybe the growth was gargantuan. The point is that every time you grew, you got better at handling the puppet and

controlling its impulses, preventing potential disaster at every turn. It has very much been like learning to ride a skateboard. After years of bloody wounds, you have turned into Tony Hawk and can perform masterful moves, even at an advanced age.

12. How does a soul grow or, in a broader perspective, how does God grow? Contrary to popular speculation, God is not a static entity. It is in and around everything you know about and everything you do not know about. The God part of you is your soul, and it grows every time you go against the grain of your ego's programming and choose love, pure unadulterated unconditional love.

13. Love can't be separated out. Because another soul is so encased and intertwined with the body, love goes to both the character who acted against the soul and the poor soul who wasn't listened to. They will both receive it when they are open and willing to do so. Gifts of love are never wasted. They will wait under the Christmas tree indefinitely. Eventually, it is the goal that the soul and the body will merge in a unified manner and become a singular entity of the eternal, expressing full time through a temporary form. Until that point, creating more of God, creating more love is messy. The ego's resistance will guarantee it.

14. If there were a singular human ego on the earth, it would be easier for it to find its way out of the fog of human thinking. With billions of egos over thousands of years, the energy of all of those brains has created its own stratosphere and thinking any other way is next to impossible. Egos can be nice, but something usually has to be in it for them. Egos can also take the opposite extreme and be absolutely vicious. No one is safe around those with bitterness in their hearts. Most egos fluctuate somewhere in the middle where it is safer. Self-preservation is first and foremost, so protecting itself from the myriad of dangers out there is high on the list of priorities.

15. In the illusion of being a human vs. being a soul aspect of God, the ego feels a very real sense of danger due to the threat posed by others. The ego feels alone and separate from all other egos except for those connected through familial or tribal commonalities. Having some common purpose is key in these special alliances. Having common enemies is another.

16. The second dilemma is Whole vs. Special. The ego is not real. It is completely unaware that it is merely a temporary mechanism for soul growth. Therefore, the ego is anything but whole. An integrated body-soul would be united and would produce a whole entity, a holy entity, since the soul is part of God, part of the source of everything. Because none of this applies to 99.99 percent of humans, we must look at what does apply to them, which is specialness.

17. Specialness is how the ego evaluates itself and everyone else. It is a broad umbrella term that houses or categorizes. It can be both positive and negative. Someone can be cast into a category and remain there or can shift from positive to negative or vice versa. Someone who has been cast out can worm their way back in with showers of gifts and affection. The same person can be kicked to the curb if they fail to deliver the goods or fail to adequately compete with a third party who is vying for someone's attention and/or affection.

18. Specialness is the name of the game here and it is bred from competition. The ego searches for others who will be loyal to it and will reward this loyalty. Virtually all friendships, business partnerships, and so-called love relationships are based on specialness, not on wholeness, not unconditional love and acceptance.

19. In the illusion that human thinking produces, characters believe tooth and nail that they are real and reinforce each other's realness or their belief in it. They believe in all sorts of things, but the truth of them being part of God operating their bodies is beyond comprehension. They

believe their name is Bob or Suzie and that they have a past and a potential future. They have likes and dislikes, regrets, and hopes. They may believe in tradition, the importance of education, religion, or none of the above.

20. Because their thinking is so limited, they aren't able to grasp the big picture and their part in it. They are products of personality and how much intelligence they have or do not have.

21. Religiously oriented ones may attend Sunday services in their childhood church or a similar one nearby. They may pray to a God for needs or special favors. They may ask for help with a situation or with a need for physical healing. They hold onto hope when all else fails. Because they don't understand the human condition to begin with, they just hold onto hope and grasp at straws. As the Bible says, "They know not what they do."

22. The purpose of human life has varied from person to person, from society to society. People try to achieve something that they think contributes in some small way, but the daily grind is too much for too many. Self-destructive behaviors, physical and mental illness, and a lack of basic necessities, such as food and housing, mar the landscape, while a select few share the majority of the world's wealth and resources. Where is the fairness in this situation? What can a purposeless purpose of acquiring more property, wealth, and status possibly say, other than "Help!" Where has God been in the worldscape? If God is everywhere, has God been present but powerless to change anything? It may startle you to read my answer, which is yes. God has been powerless here until now.

23. There are two truths about God in the world. The first is that God is everywhere and that there is nowhere God isn't to be found. The second is that the strength or potency of God on the earth is still relatively weak, whereas the strength of the ego is extremely strong, off the charts strong.

With this understanding, one can see what the main problem is here.

24. Making God stronger is a complicated affair. It isn't as simple as joining a church or subscribing to a list of beliefs. It isn't about praising God more or praising the one incorrectly thought of as his one and only son (me). None of these things will strengthen God one iota because God is not inside a church. God is inside of you and everyone you know and don't know. God is inside those who are thought to be evil incarnate and those who walk the earth as saints.

25. How does one change something that has no cohesive sense of purpose to something that does? How can the reality of God being here be reflected here in power and majesty? As it is now, the great life-force itself plays second fiddle to the whims and desires of creatively thinking robots. Let's return to the initial intent of the earth project. It was always intended as an intense pressure cooker to create more God energy by having all characters one day realize that they have been tricked into believing they are something that they are not. This is known as awakening, which is the opposite of being asleep or living in a dreamlike state. One can live on the earth in an illusionary or dreamlike state, or one can live on the earth in degrees of being awake. Everything from 4:00 a.m. grogginess to ultimate awareness is possible. Now is the time for the latter. After millennia of illusion, now is the time for ultimate awareness about your true identity and what is truly going on here.

26. This is *Soul in the Driver's Seat: A Course in Miracles for Today*. Unless you're okay with the confusion of not knowing who you really are and why you're here in a world of form, this is required reading. If you're okay with the status quo, this will be required reading for you when you're ready, and that time will be sooner rather than later. For the vast majority of people, now is the time to start a new adventure, which will lead to another new adventure, which will lead to another new adventure. All of which will peel away layers and layers of illusionary

thought and will allow more and more of the true you to shine through. Be ready for tears. Be ready for laughter. Be ready to be confronted so you can take a hard look at what you have made, keep what is real, and allow what is illusionary to fade away – all while the real you gets stronger in the process.

Chapter Three

Revelations

1. The first revelation is that the power of God, the power of a soul, is trapped and is unable to express through dense matter. The God who is prayed to in the nether regions is not far away but cannot express and be listened to until it learns how to perform this difficult task. This soul is surrounded by others who are at the same level of development and maturity, so they are in the same boat.

2. God is cursed when it is seen as being punishing and is praised with gratitude when it is seen as kind and generous. But the reality of the situation is that God is not a major player in any situation. Life provides things and situations that characters like, and life provides things and situations that characters do not like at all. They are typically attributed to God but have little to do with Him/Her/It/Them. What is this life-force that I speak of? You can think of it as an external system responsible for the growth of souls from seed to full, unbridled expression. It provides everything of a positive nature, just as sunlight, water, and soil provide everything needed for the growth of a regular seed. Where do all of the negative aspects of life come from? They come from the characters themselves. When they resist their own soul's call to express love, small to large disasters await.

3. Think of the life-force as something that organizes life. It has a say in personality development through astrological energy influence. It has a say in the birth order for certain characters. It has a say on family

assignment. It has a say on any developmental disorders or disabilities that an individual soul or a family of souls will be dealing with. By default, the life-force knows who will be born into wealth, middle-class comfort, or extreme poverty. All of this and much more is in the realm of the life-force, which deals in odds and likelihoods to bring about the desired conditions for soul development. Everything, and I mean everything, has to do with the number one objective and priority for the life-force: soul development.

4. With this explained, there is a plethora of events and situations that trigger what the life-force knows as Plan B.

5. The exercise of free will is the single most important element when creating something eternal, which is defined as something that cannot be altered by time and is not temporary. Characters say no all the time. They go left instead of right or right instead of left. They choose things that may cause harm. They choose things that may cause short- or long-term suffering for themselves and others. The list is endless because egos are primarily selfish. When egos pull their characters away from the flow that the life-force wants to take them in, then the life-force itself has to recalibrate and come up with a Plan B. Plan Bs are never as good as Plan As. They always involve making lemonade out of lemons. Maybe a character has long-repressed feelings related to trauma incurred somewhere along the way and then developed a dependency on alcohol for self-medication purposes. Let's say the character had a DUI charge and spent time in jail. This is definitely not a Plan A situation and is a Plan B situation. The life-force desperately wants the character back into the flow of life because it does not want a soul to be imprisoned where growth may be especially difficult. This is just one example of how the robots try to run the show. Egos desperately want to stay in the illusion. Their lives depend on it.

6. All souls want the grand and mystical illusion to end once and for all.

The illusion of separateness and independence has locked out the soul, who has had a minor part at best in the great play of life. Souls want characters to start to question their beliefs. This will have a twofold effect. The first is that one question will lead to the next and an awakening can happen. The second is that the awakening will lead to a shift in identity, a shift away from the brain to the heart, from fear to love, from me to you.

7. The third dilemma is Power vs. Powerlessness. There is very little power here and a great deal of powerlessness. Control falls in the latter category. Freedom falls in the category of power. The human robots have illusionary power within the realm of the illusion, but that's all. As hard as they will try, they do not have the ability to prevent an awakening from happening or to stop it. They only have the power to delay in time, and time itself is a powerful part of the illusion, held together by thought.

8. The ego's thought system, plus other egos' thought systems, cast an incredibly powerful spell that locks out the voice of the soul. Most can only hear it faintly. It is quiet and is overshadowed by loud ego-led voices from within and without. This isn't to say that the ego is bad, or that it doesn't do nice things from time to time when it feels especially benevolent. Egos, individually and collectively, have done wonderful things for individuals and communities in need. These prompts may have originated from the soul but had to be filtered through the ego. This process dampens the pure love inspirations somewhat, but the ego and soul can work together in harmony from time to time. The life-force uses both benevolence from the soul and fear-driven situations to advance characters to create openings. The goal here is always more care and consideration for others, more love. The problem is the mind's interference. It has the power to completely stop love. Love cannot be harmed, but it can be delayed.

9. The ego by itself is a problem and always has been. The ego, gently tempered and guided by soul, is the first stop in the awakening process, and this stop is what the new course in miracles is promoting. If every human adult and child alike could educate themselves about the basics and then allow even a small shift from ego to heart and from fear to love to occur, the world would be a very different place indeed.

10. In order to accomplish this, we need to provide more information about the ego, the illusionary thought system, as well as information about souls and God, a commodity largely missing from the equation here. Once this is accomplished, a step-by-step process for ego deactivation and soul empowerment will be included in *Soul in the Driver's Seat: A Course in Miracles for Today*.

11. The fourth dilemma is Competition vs. Cooperation. Not all competition is harmful, but all competition is unnecessary.

12. Competition vs. Cooperation is one of the most vexing of human problems. Competition stems from an idea concerning scarcity of goods and services and can range from the ability to pay to the willingness to commit acts of bodily harm. The payoff can be physical objects, status, or reputation. The fear of losing any of these things motivates those involved to continue competitive behaviors and teach them to others, especially children. The motive for this is always to help children to do well in life and society, but this just keeps the competitive drive alive as part of the ego's trap to keep cooperation out. There are many examples of cooperation here, in the form of "you scratch my back and I'll scratch yours," but the objective is always some type of reward. Rewardless cooperation is exceedingly rare.

13. The fifth dilemma between ego and soul is Arrogance vs. Grace. The ego is arrogant about what it swears up and down that it knows, while the soul is graceful about all things, both things it has firsthand information about and things it knows nothing about. It doesn't pretend

to need to know. It's okay with not knowing and trusting that if the need were to arise, it would be informed in perfect timing. The ego, on the other hand, thinks everything and everyone revolves around it and that it must know. It believes stories that are only partially dipped in truth, and it is fine with believing falsehoods by aggrieved parties and just making things up as it goes along. As with all dilemmas, they couldn't be more different as they exist at polar opposites.

14. Two diametrically opposite thought systems and ways of being exist in every human body. One is expressed and one is suppressed, prevented from speaking and from growing. It is no wonder that the very tightly woven illusion of false identity and fear-based thought has done everything possible within its power to not allow its roommate at least equal share of the apartment. Egos know about souls, and they know about unconditional love, but see it as their responsibility to oppose them at every turn. As a consequence, from the beginning until now there is very little of God's energy on the earth in amounts significant enough to prevent many of the consequences of unbridled ego. In fact, this was part of the deal. Unconscious fear-based behavior has been allowed to reign unchecked. The life-force has had minimal ability to protect immature souls and characters from a plethora of tragedies. When you hear of someone being taken too young or for no reason, this is the result of the ego's reign of terror. Unwanted and unwelcomed things happen all the time. They are from the ego's resistance to soul and to the life-force that positively directs life's plays. Souls are never a victim, but egos frequently feel like they are. The truth is they have had something to do with creating a response to the unwanted event, and this response is the only thing within their power. The storm, the accident, and the crime were all acts in resistance to love, but the response is within the ego's realm. The sixth dilemma is Victim vs. Victor.

15. However difficult, one can never be a victim of anything if they hold the power of their response in the palm of their hand. Dorothy had no control over mean Miss Witch, the tornado, or the concussion, but she did have control over her next steps as time unfolded in the dreamlike state she was in for most of the rest of the story. When she became conscious, she brought her ability to respond positively, negatively, or in a neutral manner with her. The life-force often uses difficult characters, such as the one seen as an evil witch, to deliver its messages, lessons, and opportunities to practice the power within. Life always wants you to see that no one really has any power over you. Even if they lock you up with an hourglass to scare you about how much time you have left, you still have the key to how you will respond.

16. The seventh dilemma is Defenselessness vs. Defensiveness. The ego always watches out for things to defend against. These range from common sense things to prevent slipping in the bathtub with bare feet, to ensuring that winter ice is salted before venturing outside. But the most egregiously dangerous thing to watch out for is, by far, other ego-led puppets who could have bad intentions. They could be armed to the teeth, and you could be their "wrong place at the wrong time" target or one who has been specially focused upon. Defensiveness is the ego's gift to the character. It is a gift that keeps on giving as defensiveness and stress go hand in hand.

17. Defenselessness, on the other hand, is unfathomable to the ego. They see that all types of terrible things happen to the innocent and unsuspecting, and egos don't want to be in this group. Defenselessness is not in the cards and is off the table for the vast majority. They would rather die trying to defend themselves and theirs and at least die nobly. But what if there is a better way? What if being in an egoic state is an open invitation to things that need to be protected from? What if there is another state of being where defending oneself isn't a need? The soul

never has to be protected and never has to be defended. Nothing can happen to it, ever. It can't be sold to the devil, and it can't be harmed in any way. True defenselessness is true power. It is just one of the benefits of soul identification.

18. The eighth dilemma is Reality vs. Illusion. The world is seen and experienced through the ego, which is the body's operating system and is itself not based in truth. It is for a temporary experience in soul strengthening. That's all. As real as the character seems to be, it is only part of something designed to be dismantled so that reality can be expressed through the context of the character and the body. Reality is one hundred percent based in the fuel of the Universe and of God. It is pure love, with nothing else mixed in to dilute it. All judgment, which always stems from the ego and its lord and master, the mind, does not originate from the soul and is therefore illusionary. All unconditional love in the world stems from the soul and is reality, however little there may be at any given time.

19. The human world of characters, roles, and drama is virtually one hundred percent illusionary. But remember what I said about truth. It has to be one hundred percent true, one hundred percent of the time. Although the illusionary human world is and has always been almost at the one hundred percent level, one hundred percent of the time, it is not now. Nor has it ever been at the spiritual standard for something that is considered true. There have always been small populations, sometimes in the single digits, who live their lives with a great deal to at least some amount of soul, some amount of pure, unadulterated, and unconditional love. There are those on the earth today who live a Christed life, living as their true Self most to all of the time. If Christ means God in Mankind, and I am telling you that it does, then being at the Christ level and living a life based in reality is the goal and is the answer to many unanswered prayers.

20. The ninth dilemma is Generosity vs. Greed. Because giving and receiving are one in truth, only the ego-led mind would think of them as separate acts. The ego thinks of everything as being separate from everything else, as it does seem to be. The reality of the situation seems quite implausible, whereas a soul is part of God and is connected to all other parts of God. Again, there are two things unfolding simultaneously. Souls are asking to be acknowledged and heard while egos turn a blind eye. The ego can be very generous indeed, but there is always an angle, something that it seeks, something it wants in return, even if it is just a pat on the back or a favor to cash in at a later date. Souls, on the other hand, grow stronger with each selfless act, none of which ever have to be repaid in any way.

21. The tenth and final dilemma is Grandeur vs. Grandiosity. Try as it might, the ego can never achieve true grandeur. The best that it can do is pretend. Pretense or an air of fakeness describes grandiosity. The soul doesn't pretend to be anything other than what it is. It is the real deal. It is grand and spectacular. And when it is allowed to flourish it makes itself known.

22. Summary of the Ten Ego Dilemmas or choices:

1. Fear vs. Love
2. Whole vs. Special
3. Power vs. Powerlessness
4. Competition vs. Cooperation
5. Arrogance vs. Grace
6. Victim vs. Victor
7. Defenselessness vs. Defensiveness
8. Reality vs. Illusion
9. Generosity vs. Greed
10. Grandeur vs. Grandiosity

Chapter Four

Putting It All Together: Vexing Questions

1. Some years ago, it was fashionable in some circles to wear brightly colored bracelets emblazoned with the letters WWJD, which stands for What Would Jesus Do? I'm not in your shoes but your soul is. Your soul is your true self. Your soul is the real you. The objective is to begin listening to it and allowing it to express who you really are through your assigned body and character. The ego be damned. It can move to the backseat to find out what being relegated to a second-class citizen is like. It is time for the soul to take center stage for the first time. Having an ego is not a bad thing. It has been a necessary thing as no one could function without one, but now is the time for the great shift from fear to love, from me to us. There is nothing to lose and everything to gain. In this chapter of the book, let's look at some commonly distressing issues in the world today. Let's look at them through the eyes of the soul, through love.

2. Our approach in this course will be to apply either new or revised knowledge to the context of the world, the same one all readers will be very familiar with since everyone has spent every day of their current lifetime here on the great and magical planet earth.

3. Each of the ten dilemmas will be explored within the context of both major and minor issues that humans face. In doing this type of work, readers will be able to better identify responses from the soul level and reactions from the ego level. The differences will be glaringly stark.

The differences between love and fear are not always apparent, so this type of work will help all practitioners of this craft to choose love much more often.

Relationships

4. It is first and foremost the relationship one has with oneself that is the most important determiner in factors that are part of its relationship to others. In all ten dilemmas between ego and soul, it is the dominant one that will play out in all relationships. If the dominant operating system is ego, then fear, being special, feeling powerless, competition, arrogance, victimhood, defensiveness, illusionary thought, greed, and grandiosity will be the recurring themes. If the dominant operating system is soul, then love, being whole, being powerful, cooperative, graceful, being responsible for all of one's thoughts and behavior, being defenseless, living in reality (having real thoughts), being generous, and expressing grandeur will be the recurring themes. It has always been a choice between the two, although most do not realize it is a moment-to-moment choice.

5. The reality-based purpose for all relationships, whether it is child to parent, employee to employer, or friend to friend, is in wholeness only. One presents oneself not as a broken self but a complete and whole one, not as one who seeks completion in another but one who seeks nothing but the joy that two or more wholes can experience in togetherness. It is not "I'm ok, you're ok," it is "I Am perfect, as are you who is before me." We are the accomplished. We are the Divine that isn't hard to find because we are here in this place.

6. This description of relationship and of a soul-based identity is exceedingly rare, and yet it is available to all. It is available to those who dare to question the status quo.

7. Imagine a soul-based relationship. Imagine how different it would be.

A soul-based person would not look for someone to complete them, as they are already whole and accomplished. All relationships would simply be in enhancement mode. Two or more parties would be perfect as they are, by themselves, but together they are enhanced. A soul-based person can even be in a relationship to an ego-based person who sees themselves in very different terms. They could see themselves as broken or as a victim, and yet their soul is enhanced with an energetically-charged soul-based person sitting beside them. When it comes down to it, all relationships are an exchange of positive or negative electrical charges. It is the soul-based person who is providing positive electrical charges to all of those it is in relationship with or just walks past. It's that powerful.

8. A soul-based relationship among peers is fearless. A soul-ego relationship may contain fear stemming from the dominant ego, but it is negated while in the presence of the dominant soul. This being said, all types of relationships are enhanced by the power of soul. Since soul is God, it can be said that God alters all relationships it is involved in. Most human relationships may have niceness involved, but there is typically not any substantial amount of God's energy, so the relationship will always have the possibility of being rocky or completely disastrous.

9. Applying this to human reality, there is inherent suffering involved in human relationships of all types. How could there not be? The suffering does have the capacity to point people to the other way of being in the world, the hidden way, and create space for questioning. What would soul-based parenting and other types of relationships look like?

10. The first relationship with another human is with a parental figure. We refer to them as mentors and the relationship is mentor-mentee. If the parent is soul dominant, they can guide developing egos without using fear tactics such as punishment. Loving guidance includes the use of natural consequences. A child can choose choice A or choice B, but choice B may not include any positive incentives. A mentor always

shows love and respect for the developing ego in a child and never withdraws affection no matter what behavior is exhibited or not exhibited. There are children being born into the world now with fully mature souls. Their mentors may or may not be soul dominant, so these relationships are holy or whole from the very beginning, or they may be mentee-mentor, with the child falling into the latter category.

11. Imagine if there were no fear present in an employer-employee relationship. No fear of getting fired and losing pay and benefits, no fear of being demoted to a less desirable position or shift, no fear of being investigated and getting into trouble, no fear of being falsely accused, no fear of anything because souls only seek out opportunities to serve. They don't hold onto situations that don't serve. They are happy to let them go until life gives them a new assignment to serve in.

12. Likewise, a soul-dominant employer will help a soul-dominant employee to thrive and meet their goals in the context of employment. A soul-dominant employer will help an ego-dominant employee to release fear and express love more often.

13. Soul-dominant employees with ego-dominant employers is a typically difficult situation because these types of employees will not be subscribers to a competitive office culture and will be viewed in a negative light.

14. Loyalty is conditional and is one element that is absent from a friend type of soul relationship. Unconditional love is just that, unconditional. It doesn't want or need anything from anyone. Soul-dominant individuals may enjoy going to see a movie or a concert with anyone at any level of soul development, but they are less interested in the activity than they are just being and sharing with a soul. Mentors enjoy being with other mentors and with mentees alike. They don't have to be with those of like mind, and it is better if they aren't. Soul-dominant journeymen and women are in such high need. They need to be an example with those who need an example. Mentors won't get their feelings hurt if a mentee

finishes with them and ends their relationship. One mentor may not cut it for many of the high-need characters out there. They may need many mentors before they are ready to graduate to the next level.

15. There are many types of human relationships besides the three broad categories we've talked about, but are there really? On one hand, in regard to the ego, there are. We didn't mention sworn enemy relationships, "I hope I never set eyes on you again" relationships, abuser-abused relationships, popular-unpopular relationships. This list is a lengthy one. These relationships do not exist when at least one party is soul dominant, because the relationships are always among equals. No one has the upper hand because that type of thinking does not exist with souls, whose thinking is always done with the Christ Mind and involves equality and sharing of everything that can be shared.

Health and Wellness

16. The dilemma between power and powerlessness is seen in the strongest sense in the category of health and wellness of the body. It is truly a vexing problem. Getting a mild to major illness or developing any type of condition is part of the human condition. It is part of being human and no one escapes. Whether it is a stomachache, headache, muscle tear, cough, cold, the flu, Covid, or many different types of cancer, the list is seemingly endless.

17. Humans are powerless and don't know from one day to the next what sickness or health malady awaits them. They try to turn the tables and buy time by staving off things that will rob them of health, of feeling good, of feeling happy, without a care in the world. They exercise, take vitamins, go in for preventative checkups, eat the right foods in the right amounts, and avoid the wrong foods in any amount. And yet people die of lung cancer who have never smoked, and people die at young ages who are champions of fitness and healthy eating, whereas people who

make questionable food choices may live to one hundred, along with smokers and alcohol enthusiasts.

18. Eating nutritious food and exercising aren't bad things. They may contribute to longevity, but are they significant contributors? Returning to the ten dilemmas, can you see that the ones associated most strongly with dominant ego would have a price tag associated with them? I am here to suggest to you that these ten items are the strongest things that work against health and wellness. On the other hand, the ten items that are most closely aligned with soul promote health and wellness. The bottom line is that thoughts that are even remotely fear related keep ego-dominant individuals trapped in the illusion of being human exclusively, while soul-based identity counteracts that and produces health and wellness as a result.

19. Merely having regular run-of-the-mill human thoughts, which are illusionary thoughts, makes one susceptible to disease, which is a state of being ill at ease. This is what the word disease or dis-ease means. While it may seem possible that doing this and that, or not doing that or this, may be effective in preventing disease from arriving at your doorstep, it's futile when it comes right down to it. Maybe a vaccination can prevent a specific disease from visiting a specific vaccinated person, but if the dominant thoughts remain from their host, the ego, other diseases will wait in the wings. Medical technology can cure many conditions and stop them in their tracks, but no one has figured out what the real culprit is.

20. Advances in medical technologies have saved and extended countless lives. They have given people more time, and many who have been given more time have shifted their programming and have made room for their soul to express love. Some comment, "It's not the same person," after someone they know has had a bout with cancer or some other life-threatening disease. These situations have the power to help someone

change their priorities and change the road they've been traveling on. Without medicine this gift of additional time would not be able to be given, and time is needed for soul growth. Egos produce diseases that create pain and suffering in the now, the only time there is.

Time

21. Where is the past that is so often referred to? Where can one locate it? While we are at it, where is the future? Can you get into a car or an airplane and go to these places? Time is not like a book where you can turn back to an earlier chapter and see what a character's childhood was like or skip ahead and see what a disaster a character's wedding reception is going to be. The past and the future live in the brain, which has attached memories to artifacts from a time passed by or an aspirational future. The lamp grandma gave me before she died triggers all of my memories about grandma. These memories are all in the past, a past that lives only in the brain. It doesn't even live inside a tombstone. The tombstone serves as a reminder to those who knew grandma on some level. To those who walk by in the cemetery it may mean nothing. They can only imagine what her life must have been like based on the time period she lived in and how many children and other family members she left behind.

22. Time is illusionary and yet it isn't. If there is only *now*, then that means there has been an extensive and vast collection of *past nows*. The proof is in the pudding. You were once a baby learning to walk. The connected *nows* make a chain that can be called the past. Your body has aged as has the tree in the backyard. Your brain remembers the chain of *past nows*, and your own body is an artifact of living time. It didn't always look the way it does now. And yet you can't go backwards in time. Time is illusionary. Two people may have very different sets of memories about the same event they both experienced together, side

by side. Their own brains recorded the *now* differently based on their own perceptions. Over time the chain of *past nows* fades. You may have an award ceremony photograph without any memory of having been there to receive the award. What about the future?

23. The future rests its head on a concept known as *if this, then that*. It is a wished outcome scenario of likelihoods. A character may hope that one day they will be rich after winning a lottery. Then they can retire, play golf, and live a life of ease. Less wishful thinking characters can hope to make it through college to earn a degree and then settle down to start a family. Futures typically ask for planning and completing needed steps for a likely outcome. This method has worked for many. They did, in fact, receive a basic framework of a projected plan in a *past now*. They did become a hairdresser who opened their own shop in suburban Chicago, but they also received plenty of things they did not plan for.

24. Characters receive what they have told themselves that they want at times, and at other times they receive what they did not want, things that no one wants. Characters then start to plan on ways to prevent the unwanted things from appearing again, while at the same time never forgetting the times in *past nows* when they received something unwanted and undesirable. This is how most humans experience the *now* time, the only time there is. They don't fully experience it. It is just a bridge between a past filled with faulty memories and a projected future filled with things they want and not things they don't want. Add to this the attributes of the ten ego dilemmas and you can discover how problematic human life is, and how different it is from a soul-based life.

Sex

25. Because the ego does not feel as if it is complete, sharing physical intimacy with others is a treasured experience. Beyond reproductive

purposes, the simple act of touching and being touched gives not only the ego, but the soul as well, a deep feeling of connection with another. While there have been many books written about the spiritual or tantric side to sex, my purpose in writing this section of this new book is to explore the topic through the context of the ten ego dilemmas.

26. Where does the sex drive come from? Is it primarily for reproductive purposes? Is this why there is a sex drive to begin with? The answer may surprise you, but the answer is no. Reproduction may be a benefit of the sex drive depending on the situation, but it isn't the primary purpose. The primary purpose is for substitution. The ego is wanting to duplicate a sense of unity that was lost when the soul seemingly left a state of unity to be in the world of form. Sex acts of all types are largely reinforcing, and the human is a creature of habit. Over time, sex became a primary motivator and need. The drive for sex is stronger than the drive for food or sleep in many people, but let's not forget that in most cases it is ego driven. Many of the ten ego dilemmas play out in this conflict-ridden area.

27. There may be a great deal of guilt associated with this topic, but it isn't the sex itself that creates this. It is all of the thoughts that surround sex and have attached themselves to it that created the guilt. Children may have been told that masturbation is wrong and then felt shame surrounding it. Teenagers may have been taught that sex is only for traditionally married couples and may feel shame if they don't wait for marriage or don't even want to get married. So why should they wait? A young married couple may have been taught that sexual intimacy is only for procreation and may feel shame about intimacy while using birth control. Committed couples may feel incredible amounts of guilt if they have sexual encounters outside of their primary relationship if both parties have not explicitly agreed to this. Gay men and lesbians have their own hurdles to jump over involving defining what sex means

to them, and then having to explain it to family members who may not approve. This minefield of a topic covers numerous dilemmas but none as much as fear vs. love.

28. If an innocent desire by an adult to touch another consenting adult is perceived fearfully, then various judgments get attached to it. "You can't do that." "You shouldn't do that." "That is wrong." "God won't like you if you even think about doing that." This is where shame and guilt come into play, but they don't have to and never had to throughout time. The ego made this decision when it came up with religious ideas steeped in the desire to control the populace. If we strip away all fear from the simple desire to touch and be touched, then the topic of sex can be demystified.

29. We've covered external and internalized judgments about sex through the eyes of fear. Now let's talk about how other dilemmas can play out.

30. The ego can turn any simple and innocent desire into something as dangerous as a weapon. Sex is frequently used as a weapon of control. There are those who refuse it unless they get what they want first. There are those who will force it on an unwilling partner as a way to punish them. There are those who demand it and threaten with blackmail unless their request is granted. The reality of a loving desire to make love is frequently cast into the illusion by characters who want to use others for their own purposes. Of all the subcategories in this chapter of vexing problems, sex is by far the most problematic.

Death

31. You can't blame anyone for the fear of death. There could be a tremendous amount of suffering and pain involved. Sometimes it is announced that death may pay someone a visit soon, and sometimes a death is a completely unexpected shock. Some never recover from the death of a loved one. They miss their presence and may have guilt about

things that were done or things that were not said.

32. Because humans don't see the big picture and don't know about their true identity, death doesn't seem like a passage as much as it seems like a cruel joke. Babies die. Children die. People die in the prime of their life. People die who are expected to. And people die unexpectedly.

33. If the human identity and the thoughts that go along with it create this vast illusion, then how can death be true?

34. Death is as much a reality here as birth is, but if you aren't really a character with a body, then can you die, and can death be ultimately real? The answer is a resounding no. You are the energy that activates the body and presents itself as a character, but you are not either of those things. When the body dies and the character is laid to rest, it's just as if a book has closed with many more waiting to be written. Death can be seen in a more celebratory light, but it won't be until the truth of everyone's identity becomes more widely known. Different ego dilemmas play out around the death of characters, and there is a great deal of fear that surrounds it. Do some go to heaven? Do some go to hell? Do some just fade away?

35. The truth is that the real you never dies. It never has and it never will, although it has experienced the death of all of its characters as an observer. Death of a character just signals an exit from earth time and an entrance into time outside of time where you are reunited with souls who played your character's friends and enemies. All of these souls are strengthened from the experience of expressing love through a character who may not have been too keen on it. Some of you may have grown considerably in this one group of lifetimes and others may not have. But every one of God's souls will play another day, so to speak, and will be assigned new characters to play in the great drama that is life.

Money

36. Money is something that controls most lives to a large degree. Do I have enough? How long will it last? What happens if I run out? Do I have to keep working at a job I hate just to pay the basic bills? What happens if I get sick or need surgery and I don't have insurance? Do I have enough for diapers and formula? The list goes on and on. Money usually dictates how people feel about themselves. If there isn't enough, people may feel like they can't afford to be generous. People who have more than enough may feel like they have to hang on to what they have and even stockpile it. Generosity vs. Greed and Grandeur vs. Grandiosity are at play in this area.

37. If a character finds themselves in a low-wage job with less than full-time hours, they may question their life choices to get married and not attend college. Money is seen as a necessity and as a reward for hard work. The ten dilemmas as seen through ego make characters feel powerless and trapped. They wish they could choose love and see things differently, but when there are bills to be paid and mouths to feed, love seems like a pipe dream, an unwise choice.

Relationships Revisited

38. A singular human being is in relationship to everything and everyone. The people who make bread at the factory for morning toast, the people who provide gasoline for the local gas station, and the people who read the news from teleprompters are all in relationship with millions of people they will never meet. One false move by anyone and jobs can end, and relationships can be altered or broken.

39. Humans have relationships with ideas. They may hate certain ideas, so the relationship is one of rejection. They may like or approve of certain ideas, so these relationships are of acceptance. These ideas help to codify self-image and group identity. They indicate that an individual is a

certain type, who likes specific things and hates, or at least dislikes, certain other things. These ideas can and often do attach themselves to objects. You can wear a T-shirt emblazoned with an idea you support, or you can speak at a school board meeting about objects such as books that promote ideas you disapprove of. A single human has more relationships with ideas and objects than they do with other humans.

40. People have relationships with brand names. They can never drink coffee that doesn't come from brand X. They will never wear sneakers other than the ones from a certain brand. They only wear specific styles and colors because they have relationships with them. These relationships affect how people see themselves and how they hope to be seen by others. Even people who live off the grid are in relationship to entire lists of ideas about themselves. Maybe they are anti-government and pro-militia. Maybe they don't trust anyone or anything. Here's a question. What do you think would happen if you took a single human being and stripped all ideas away? What would you be left with?

41. Why does the ego feel like it has to define itself? Are these defining thoughts ways to make it seem special and important? This is how the dilemma of Grandeur vs. Grandiosity plays out. Everything, and I mean everything, the ego does is to make the character seem as if it has value. It may be educated, have certain beliefs, done things it feels are important, or received awards. At the other end of the spectrum, it may have gone to jail, hunted lions, or rubbed elbows with someone it feels is important. All of this is grandiosity, plain and simple. It only has value because an unreal operating system of the body says it does, and perhaps other egos agree with it or at least they say they do. Do you see how illusionary all of this is now?

42. What is left when you strip away all of the ideas, concepts, should haves, would haves, and could haves? This is where the soul lives. Soul is beneath thought and covered over by it. This is where God lives. This

is reality. This is the real world. The soul or God seeks to surpass thought and the illusion it creates in order to create relationship first and foremost with the body. When the body has been consumed by soul, the soul then seeks to consume already established relationships and creates new ones on a mentor-mentee level and on a peer level of mentor-mentor. This is, and always has been, the purpose and goal of this and all worlds of form.

Criminality and Evil

43. At this point, you can see the connection between the ego and a myriad of fear-based behaviors, including criminality and what has been referred to as evil acts. Some behavior can be explained away. Maybe someone was beaten or bullied as a child. Some behavior is so horrific that it simply can't be explained. Things happen here every minute of every day that produce revulsion. They increase fear and make the illusion of thought even thicker.

44. A singular criminal act such as theft may or may not include an evil intent to take away property or harm someone. Either way, the act stems from fear. These acts occur at times when the ego is in revenge mode. Egos can be quite dangerous. If they feel that their needs are not now and/or have not ever been met, great harm can come to others in the illusion, meaning the human experience that is void of soul to a large degree. Egos lash out at known nearby targets mostly but can also lash out in the larger collective against complete strangers, as you see in the newer phenomenon of mass shootings. The phrase *fear begat fear* is absolutely true as the acts of a lone ego will forever alter the lives that are directly and indirectly impacted. There is even a third group here – the ones who read about incidents or see them on television. This group is in the multimillions. Their defenses and desires to defend are highlighted with every new incident of small-to-large proportion.

45. There isn't a celestial being somewhere who inspires evil loveless acts and wants them to happen with greater and greater frequency. Egos, all by themselves, are responsible for all the terrible things that happen in the world. They are by definition and design, loveless beings. Therefore, just by being in this illusionary loveless-by-design world, literally anything can happen at any time. The ego offers no protection. God would protect itself if there were more of it in greater strengths. In the illusionary if-this-then-that world, many things happen that go against plan. Lives are lost and others are forever altered by things like being in the wrong place at the wrong time. This is part and parcel of the illusionary thought that created the human world to begin with. The reality of love and the concept of *as within, so without* don't materialize until the container of the ego, the body's lord and master, starts to allow it.

46. Punishing criminal and evil acts has done virtually nothing to diminish them. Being a criminal can be a shameful act or it can be an identity: a point of pride. There are gang members who target people they think are wealthy, can afford the loss they are about to endure, and perhaps deserve what is about to happen to them.

47. In the illusion of human thought there are degrees of like but there is very little, if any, unconditional love. The illusion is not eternal and not based in love. We say that it does not meet the definition of real or reality, and yet it is very real in its own way according to its own established rules. It is very much an alternative reality. It is more real than putting on a headset and playing an artificial intelligence game because you can feel pain and experience hardship. The human world is an illusionary alternative reality with real blood and guts to prove it. The question is, what purpose does it have?

Thought

48. As you can see thus far, it is thought itself that got humankind into this mess. It is the mother of all vexing problems. Thought creates illness of all types. Thought creates problematic reactions to problematic reactions to problematic reactions. It is a vicious circle. This is where we will end this chapter of the book. The next chapter will take a look at other factors at play within the illusion.

Chapter Five

Healing

1. What is it exactly that needs to be healed here? Where would one even start? Let's say that I entered any hospital in the world and went room to room, healing this one of this disease and the next one of another disease and yet another of something else. Then what would happen? Maybe John and Mary Smith could go back home to be John and Mary Smith, illusionary characters in an illusionary world of thought, where they will then be free to create new diseases for themselves just by thinking like a human. So again, what is it exactly that needs to be healed here? If you are saying human thought and human identity you are right on the button. How can these things change? Through the miracle, that's how. A change in perception.

2. Diseases of all shapes and sizes are merely symptoms of a much larger disease, the disease of separation! Separation between one soul and another and more importantly, separation between a soul and God, are part of perception, part of the soul-strengthening exercise of being in a world of form. As I've already indicated it isn't true, and yet it definitely seems to be true according to the parameters of this experience. In the original *A Course in Miracles*, I took a hardliner's stance about this and may have done harm by instilling guilt about being a human in the first place. For this, I sincerely apologize. In this new version, I will attempt to be clear when speaking of your ultimate reality as well as your current reality.

3. People are healed of both temporary and life-threatening disease either through medical intervention, wishful thinking, or a third avenue, bargaining with God and making promises to be good if "fill in the blank" will disappear. Disease takes people out of their daily routine and forces them to focus on being sick right now. Through suffering, oftentimes horrific suffering, people have a required time-out and sometimes reevaluate their life's purpose and their relationships to their careers, family, and friends. This is one potentially positive takeaway from health issues if one digs for a deeper meaning. A pitfall is if the star of a sick show becomes focused on leaving a painful now through the use of painkillers. This creates a brand-new problem and an escape hatch from dealing with the hidden messages the disease comes to deliver in the first place.

Chapter Six

Religion

1. What would life on earth be like without religion? There are many humanists and atheists who live largely religion-free lives. I say largely because it is quite difficult to live here without being aware of the huge influence religion has on culture and on each individual, whether they like it or not. There are communities that voted to have gambling facilities only to have them blocked by local churches. There are places where alcohol cannot be sold because of old laws created by politicians who were being supported by religious communities, who fight tooth and nail to this day to keep them in place. America has seen school boards and an entire political party consumed by religion that practitioners want enshrined into law. What is really going on here?

2. Few have found love in religion, although there is some there, buried deeply underneath what is primarily there, which is fear and the desire to control through fear. Their purpose, other than fundraising, is to promote an idea that there is a God in the sky who watches your every move and is either pleased with your loyalty or displeased with your treason. Punishment is a big theme in religion as is redemption for sinners. If one merely believes in the Christian Savior (me), then they will either go to heaven when they die, or be swept up in a rapture, or be resurrected after one thousand years, depending on what version of the story is subscribed to. In other religions pious males will receive the reward of having seven virgin wives. I don't know what the reward for women would

be. Women frequently get left out and get the short end of the stick.

3. Very few egos feel free enough to escape the clutches of religion once they have taken hold. A decision like this could cost them business associates or family members. It is amazing that religion has survived throughout history and even supports all of the ten dilemmas between ego and soul, though always on the ego side interestingly enough. Religion is the glue that keeps the illusion firmly in place. Without it there may have been enough wiggle room for people to start questioning everything. Religion has made many feel great fear about questioning anything. If anyone is brave enough to do so, they will discover that religion is largely superstition and fables.

4. Humans are doomed. They have an archaic operating system that opposes souls at every turn. They are under the influence of drugs such as religion and government. Poor things. The souls are the ones who really suffer though. They may have to live a life that lasts for one hundred years of only being listened to a handful of times. It is as if they are locked inside a bottle and can't escape even for a breath of fresh air. Souls are the ones activating bodies, so you would think they would get a little more respect, but most people don't know much about their own soul. The ego has made sure of it and religion has only made the waters dirtier. What to do? You have read this far. Keep going. It will be worth it, I promise. You'll see.

5. If there is not much truth to be found in religion or anywhere in the world, does this mean that there isn't any at all? The answer to this question will lead to many more questions, and as I've already said, questioning is a very good thing, to partially quote Martha Stewart. The answer to the question is an enthusiastic yes. There is truth in this world, and you've already started to uncover what it is. If you aren't really human, or at least completely human, what are you? And who and what am I? Why am I talking to you now? What's my agenda?

Chapter Seven

Steps to Authenticity

Introduction

1. This is a book within a book. I am the one known as Jesus, and my agenda is the same as it was two thousand years ago. I came to teach and promote peace, love, and understanding. My message was not clearly understood and recorded. Egos did not understand someone who was not coming from a place of ego but of soul. They thought I must have been special to be so unlike them, but my message was that I wasn't special. Each and every human is a soul aspect of the totality of God. That was my message then and it remains so today. Now let's begin.

2. The agenda is a simple one. Humanity is to awaken from the insane illusion and discover what has been hiding in plain sight all along. Love is the answer to all individual and collective problems, but believing in it isn't enough. You have to be it. You have to be love in a place that is hostile to it, a place that only tolerates *like* for short periods of time. How would someone go about something as radical as this? How would they stop being one thing in order to be something else? This isn't what I'm asking you to do. I am simply asking you to be who you are in truth. I am asking you to be yourself, stripped of pretense, stripped of requirements, stripped of the need to perform, simply bare take-it-or-leave-it for all to see. I am asking you to be a loving soul who goes by your name and has your history and your

talents and your peculiarities. I am asking you to leave fear behind once and for all, starting with judgment.

3. It is a miracle if a soul speaks, is heard, and is honored by following its advice. It is a guaranteed change in perception. As with the original *A Course in Miracles*, there will be exercises offered to help strengthen the soul and weaken the grip the ego has over the character. Formerly known as the *Workbook for Students*, this chapter will now be known as "Steps to Authenticity." Instead of daily lessons, this chapter will have exercises for reflection. There will be 365 of these, precisely the same number that the original *Workbook for Students* had. Because the times have changed, the terms *teacher* and *student* will be known as *mentor* and *mentee*. A mentor is soul-dominant, and a mentee is soul-emergent.

4. This chapter weaves topic content with daily meditative Steps to Authenticity, as a demonstration of unity rather than separation. It is my hope and our hope that this book will be the living testament between the God within and all mortal aspects, who are to grow and reflect the reality of their identity. If the illusion of identity is to be changed permanently, it will take everyone's dedication. Doing so will create heaven on earth, the Kingdom of God, where heaven and earth are one state.

5. Each month offers a thorough discussion of a specific topic, followed by adequate time for daily reflection. The goal being to master the mind as soul instead of the mind mastering the soul. You will be your authentic Self after a year's worth of application, and you will not need to repeat the course. You will be ready to move on to material for mature souls: soul-dominant individuals.

6. Again, the goal is to undo the dominant thinking of the ego in favor of a more soulful and love-based approach.

7. Each month of the year will begin with a description, from the soul's

perspective, of the specified topic. The daily reflections will then help the emerging soul to achieve this perspective by whittling away the mind's viewpoints that interfere with it. A mentee may start at the beginning of any month during the calendar year and finish 365 days later.

January: Judgment

1. Our goal here is to move from constant evaluation to just observing what is. Instead of bad/good, positive/negative, hard/easy, ugly/pretty, smart/dumb, the soul uses factual language and pairs this with acceptance. Souls describe things such as yellow dress, spicy sauce, long hair, without stating that something is ugly or horrible. Even using terms like *pretty* and *smart* imply that they have an opposite. If the yellow dress is seen by an ego as ugly, cheap, or something that obviously came from a discount or thrift store, then it keeps going. Next it evaluates who would wear an ugly, cheap, yellow dress. This clothing selection must reflect the person who is wearing it. Therefore, the wearer must be poor and have bad taste. Maybe they are someone you wouldn't want to associate with.

2. All evaluative judgment is of the self. Someone may think someone is wrong about something or is stupid, when what they really worry about is their own intelligence or whether they are on the right side of an issue. The ego is all about projection. It takes its judgments about itself and throws them outward. They could land anywhere or on anyone. Everyone collects these and no one knows how to digest them. Some people have large collections of hate-filled comments and behavior that have been

directed at them. The choice seems to be to accept and believe that they are true or to turn around and throw them back at the one who tossed them in the first place. And if the person isn't available for whatever reason, the comments can be thrown at any nearby target. Egos relish venom and they especially love to watch it happen to those they think deserve it.

3. Judgment keeps humans glued to the past and to the future. That one thing someone said or did twenty years ago may be alive and well in someone's mind. They could still feel hurt by it, even though the person who said or did it is dead and gone. Feeling ridicule from the past may make someone not get back on the bike, so to speak, to ride another day, for fear of it happening again. Being less judgmental and less inclined to punish others or oneself is a way to reduce stress and start to open up to new avenues that your soul will show you through unconditional love. Here are daily reflections for January.

4. **Guidelines**: Pick a time of day that suits you best and read the step that corresponds to the appropriate month and date. This is your starting point. Simply reflect on what the step means to you and ways to put it into practice. Accept whatever feelings come to the surface as you work your way through the steps. These steps are the beginning of a transformation where love replaces fear, which is no easy feat. Be patient with yourself. You are doing what few have ever been able to do. Now you have the means. Just add a little willingness and you will be a more soulful and less ego-driven being in just a year's time. Godspeed.

5. January   1

Pick any object in the room where you currently are and describe it factually, without any added opinions about it.

6. January 2

Pick someone you have interacted with today and describe them factually, without any added opinions about them.

7. January 3

Describe yourself in factual terms (age, height, hair color, occupation), without any added opinions.

8. January 4

Pick one event in your life from the past year and describe it factually, without labeling it as good, bad, or neutral.

9. January 5

Pick one event in your distant past (more than three years ago) that was difficult for you to experience. Now take away all of the negative descriptors and just factually describe the event.

10. January 6

Pick someone who was in your life, but the relationship has since ended. Describe this relationship (including the ending) in factual terms only.

11. January 7

Revisit a time when you became aware of negative comments others made about you. Describe the comments in factual terms only.

12. January 8

Going back to these negative comments, even though they were directed towards you, take yourself out and reframe this incident. See yourself as innocent and not deserving of harm.

13. January 9

Again, going back to these negative comments, reframe the situation and see those who made the comments as innocent, as ones who mistakenly continued a chain of mistreatment that was originally directed towards them.

14. January 10

Bless those involved with this pain-filled situation and see them as whole. See their words and actions as nothing more than mistakes.

15. January 11

Make a mental note of a time when you believed that you were less than and were deserving of mistreatment.

16. January 12

See yourself as whole and complete. You are not your mistakes. You are a whole aspect of God, an ongoing work in progress.

17. January 13

Describe a song that you enjoy listening to. Does the fact that you like the song mean anything in particular about you?

18. January 14

Describe your favorite food. Does liking it have any additional meaning?

19. January 15

Describe your favorite drink. Does liking it have any additional meaning?

20. ## January 16

Describe a song or type of music that you want to turn off immediately. What is it that bothers you about it? Is the song or music bad? If so, can you reframe it?

21. ## January 17

Describe a food that you will refuse to eat. What is it that bothers you about it? Is the food bad? If so, can you reframe it?

22. ## January 18

Describe a drink that you will refuse to drink. What is it that bothers you about it? Is the drink bad? If so, can you reframe it?

23. ## January 19

Who is it who gives things and events meaning for you?

24. ## January 20

Can things and events be enjoyable or not be enjoyable, without them being part of your identity and personal history?

25. ## January 21

Pick someone from today's news cycle. Is this person good or bad based on a given description of their behavior?

26. ## January 22

Are you your behavior?

27. ## January 23

Is anyone their behavior?

28. January 24

What similarities do you have with someone the media has described as a notorious criminal?

29. January 25

Think about a time when you were angry and said unkind things in front of others. What did you learn about yourself from this incident?

30. January 26

Think about a time when you were in the presence of an angry person who said unkind things about you in front of others. How did you feel, and do you still carry these feelings?

31. January 27

Think about a time when you were in the presence of a funny person who made unkind comments about you in the form of a joke. How did you feel, and do you still carry these feelings?

32. January 28

Do you laugh at celebrities who are the butt of jokes in the media? What does this say about you?

33. January 29

Were you shamed by family members or adult authority figures as a child? Did you feel that you deserved this treatment?

34. January 30

How do you treat others in your life? Do you treat them the way you want to be treated?

35. January 31

Can you be on the lookout for how judgment manifests in your life, and learn to live without giving it more meaning than it needs to have?

February: The Body

1. The body is separate from all other bodies and all other things. It moves separately and independently. Its brain or command center has freedom of choice in what to do and how to do it. Sometimes the body seems to take control away from the brain. It may say that it is tired, hungry, thirsty, or sick. Other than these times, it just goes along with what the brain dictates. It will be pushed to its limits if the brain wants to run a marathon. It will gain weight and slow down if the brain says it wants more caloric intake and less movement. Since the body is a representation of the brain and its operating system, the ego, its importance in the illusion is bigger than warranted.

2. The body is seen as you, by all who gaze at it. It is you, whether someone knows your name or not. It is you today and will be you in ten or twenty years, if you're still around. To you, it's me, myself, and I. It has a name, a past history, and a potential future. This being said, the body has a great deal of value here in this world. It can be healthy or not so much, but it's all anyone has. It's given to you at birth and the rest is left to genetics, socioeconomic status, aptitude, intelligence, chance, and coincidence, or so it seems.

3. The original *A Course in Miracles* describes the body as a symbol of

separation and says that there is no separation in reality. It also says that each soul creates their own body in order to be separate from God. For a book that sought to get rid of guilt in its readership, it did a very good job of instilling a new type of guilt. The truth of the situation is that bodies are part of an alternative reality in this and in many other worlds of form. Bodies serve as a strengthening activity for souls to master the opposite of love, which is fear. A soul cannot be separate from God or from other souls, even if one wanted to be. It is impossible. The body itself is a magnificent work of art. It deserves great admiration because it is a vehicle for God. It helps God to grow more of itself, and for this simple reason it is a wonderful thing deserving of the utmost respect. In this book we seek to explain everything in ways that will leave no room for doubt.

4. **Guidelines**: Pick a time of day that suits you best and read the step that corresponds to the appropriate month and date. This is your starting point. Simply reflect on what the step means to you and ways to put it into practice. Accept whatever feelings come to the surface as you work your way through the steps. These steps are the beginning of a transformation where love replaces fear, which is no easy feat. Be patient with yourself. You are doing what few have ever been able to do. Now you have the means. Just add a little willingness and you will be a more soulful and less ego-driven being in just a year's time. Godspeed.

5. February 1

Is your body yours only?

6. February 2

Can your body be repurposed from self-centered to one of service?

7. February 3

What do you like about your body?

8. February 4

What do you dislike about your body?

9. February 5

Does a body say anything about the occupant?

10. February 6

Reflect on a time when you saw someone for the very first time and classified them into categories based on their apparent age, body type, and style of clothing.

11. February 7

How much thought do you give to the image your body projects to others?

12. February 8

List ways that body image has value to you.

13. February 9

Do you dress according to your own likes, or do you feel compelled to wear things that project a certain image?

14. February 10

Who decides what should or should not be worn in certain environments?

15. **February 11**

Do you value dress codes of any type?

16. **February 12**

What purpose does conformity in dress serve, and who does it ultimately serve?

17. **February 13**

What negative comments have you made about the bodies of others?

18. **February 14**

What positive comments have you made about the bodies of others?

19. **February 15**

Have you wondered about the effects any of your comments have had on the receivers of them?

20. **February 16**

If you gave a compliment about how beautiful someone is when they wear makeup and dyed hair, is it possible that this person may think they have to do these things in order to be pretty?

21. **February 17**

What other well-intentioned comments have you made that could have been received in a self-deprecating way?

22. **February 18**

What messages did you receive about your body and your appearance while growing up?

23. February 19

What behaviors do you exhibit today that are directly correlated to comments you have received throughout your lifetime about how you dress or how you do not dress?

24. February 20

What specific teachings were instilled in you about how to dress with regard to gender?

25. February 21

Do you now, or have you ever, wanted to dress or present yourself (makeup or hair style) in a way that broke the traditional norms related to gender?

26. February 22

Whether you are a parent or not, what have you taught children with male and female bodies about how they should or shouldn't present themselves?

27. February 24

As a body ages, are there different ideas or rules about how it should be dressed or shouldn't be dressed?

28. February 25

What are your ideas about nudity? When is it or isn't it okay for you?

29. February 26

When is it or isn't it okay for others to be nude?

30. **February 27**

Do those with physical disabilities have to adhere to special rules related to their body? Do missing limbs always have to be covered up so as not to upset others?

31. **February 28**

What are your feelings about mothers who nurse babies in public? If this bothers you, why?

32. **February 29** (Leap Year)

What ideas about bodies can you be free of?

March: Characters

1. Were you ever in a school play? Do you remember what it was like to learn lines and play a fictitious character? Then, at the conclusion of the play, you and the other members of the cast went to the front of the stage and took a bow. When the curtains closed, you stopped pretending to be that character and went back to being yourself. Right? Wrong, you went back to being another character, one you have more familiarity with and experience playing. You've played this character since you were small and started showing signs of personality. This character is a shell for the real you who is pretending to be the character. This is the biggest secret in the world. The "you" you have been playing is as real as Batgirl or Superman. All three of you are fictional characters.

2. How can fictional characters have anything that isn't an unreal experience? They live in comic books, on stages, and in plays. They were created in a writer's mind and then were made as real as possible by artists and actors. They live in fictitious worlds that were also created in a writer's mind. The key words here are *as real as possible*. They will never truly be real, just as all of the billions of human characters running to and fro today will never truly be real, because they only house something real. They only house something real temporarily, until they die and the soul moves on, or until the soul has grown sufficiently to merge with the body. Thus, making the soul an expression of reality and no longer an instrument of illusion.

3. As characters start to open up and question who they are, who their friends and enemies are, and what life is really all about – and the key word is real(ly) – they give their souls some breathing room, some space to expand in. Think of a root-bound houseplant. Once it receives more space the roots can expand, and growth that had been temporarily halted can resume. The character is the single most important element in the body-ego-mind-character equation, as it is the gatekeeper. Characters create experience through free will. They decide what kind of a reaction they will have towards the things life throws their way. They decide to resist or accept things ranging from easy and pleasant to extremely difficult and unpleasant. Everything, and I mean everything, asks the character these two questions: Are you sure about this? Is there another way to think about and approach this?

4. **Guidelines**: Pick a time of day that suits you best and read the step that corresponds to the appropriate month and date. This is your starting point. Simply reflect on what the step means to you and ways to put it into practice. Accept whatever feelings come to the surface as you work your way through the steps. These steps are the beginning of a transformation where love replaces fear, which is no easy feat. Be patient

with yourself. You are doing what few have ever been able to do. Now you have the means. Just add a little willingness and you will be a more soulful and less ego-driven being in just a year's time. Godspeed.

5. March 1

What are some positive achievements your character has accomplished thus far in this lifetime?

6. March 2

What are some negative experiences your character has experienced thus far in this lifetime?

7. March 3

Returning to your character's positive achievements, how much was your soul involved in these?

8. March 4

Returning to your character's negative experiences, how much did your soul help you to process them?

9. March 5

Think about your birth family. How much did characters in this group help you to learn more about your soul and how to allow its free expression?

10. March 6

Think about your chosen family. How much did characters in this group help you to learn more about your soul and how to allow its free expression?

11. ## March 7

Try to remember a time when you reacted from your ego to harsh circumstances. How could your soulful response have improved the outcomes?

12. ## March 8

Try to remember a time when you responded from your soul to a harsh set of circumstances. How did this help to save the day and make lemonade out of lemons?

13. ## March 9

Describe a character from your current life experience with whom you have had a terrible relationship.

14. ## March 10

Describe a character from your current life experience with whom you have had a rocky (good/bad mixture) relationship.

15. ## March 11

Returning to the terrible relationship from March 9, what was your takeaway from this experience?

16. ## March 12

Returning to the rocky relationship from March 10, what was your takeaway from this experience?

17. ## March 13

What character traits do you see as being important contributors for society?

18. **March 14**

What character traits do you see as being dangerous for society?

19. **March 15**

What character traits do you have that you consider to be important?

20. **March 16**

What character traits do you have that you consider to be potentially dangerous?

21. **March 17**

How do you enhance your important character traits?

22. **March 18**

How do you shine light on your own traits that you see as potentially dangerous?

23. **March 19**

Are you willing to see yourself in others instead of seeing them as other?

24. **March 20**

Are negative character traits really traits or are they just built-in tendencies to resist love, to resist the soul?

25. **March 21**

What character traits were taught to you as you grew up?

26. **March 22**

Which of these traits were positive?

27. March 23

Which of these traits were negative tendencies?

28. March 24

Which character traits do you value the most?

29. March 25

As you look back on your past experiences, when were there times that you felt compelled to react from your built-in programming (ego)?

30. March 26

As you look back on your past experiences, when were there times when you went out on a ledge and responded in ways that did not feel natural to you?

31. March 27

Comparing the reflections from March 25 and March 26, which reaction or response felt more joyful even if somewhat more uncomfortable?

32. March 28

Look back on a recent lunch or dinner gathering with friends. Can you tell who is reacting from ego and who is responding from soul?

33. March 29

Look back at a recent time when you observed yourself reacting from ego. What could you do differently the next time?

34. **March 30**

    Take a mental snapshot of your family as you were growing up. What was dominant in the household: ego or soul?

35. **March 31**

    The more you choose soul and love, the stronger it gets inside you and the easier it will be to repeat this choice. Can you commit to exploring your soul as a loving response more often?

April: Role-Playing

1. Characters in the earth drama play roles, just as actors play roles on TV and in films. There is no difference except that some of the actors are paid large amounts of money. Characters are another aspect of the human illusion, as is role-playing. The character thinks it is real, and role-playing helps to confirm this in the mind. Characters play the roles of oldest child, the one who does well in school, the one who can't do anything right, the leader of the team, the pretty one, the nerd, the athlete, the strict parent, the permissive parent, the one who isn't good with money – the list is endless. Someone could play several different roles in one day. It is tiring to contemplate it, but that's what characters do. It is why human relationships are so fragile. Ego-dominant individuals depend on others they are in relationship with to play their roles to hold the relationship in place. Even relationships are part of the illusion.

2. There is a phrase in the collective that is being used more and more and is taking on meaning for more and more ego-driven characters.

The phrase is "let's get real" or "keeping it real." This is a way that more and more characters are discovering how fake others are when they are strictly role-playing, or when they themselves are caught up in the illusionary web of role-playing. They feel like they can't be honest unless they break away from the trap of thoughts and move to more heart-based feelings. Remember, ego or soul is a moment-to-moment choice. But if realness is part of someone's mantra, it can help to remind a character to be real more often.

3. Role-playing is always done from ego, and therefore the ten dilemmas are at play. Soul has no use for any kind of playing or pretending, as souls only serve with love. Some of the ego-level dilemmas that make themselves known are being special, pretending to be powerful but actually being powerless, being arrogant, being defensive, being greedy, and being grandiose. Being nice falls in the latter category. Playing a character and role-playing are forced on all who come here. That is, until they start to listen to the soul and realize that there just might be another way.

4. **Guidelines**: Pick a time of day that suits you best and read the step that corresponds to the appropriate month and date. This is your starting point. Simply reflect on what the step means to you and ways to put it into practice. Accept whatever feelings come to the surface as you work your way through the steps. These steps are the beginning of a transformation where love replaces fear, which is no easy feat. Be patient with yourself. You are doing what few have ever been able to do. Now you have the means. Just add a little willingness and you will be a more soulful and less ego-driven being in just a year's time. Godspeed.

5. April   1

What has been the hardest element about the roles you have played in this current lifetime?

6. **April 2**

What has been the easiest element about the roles you have played in this current lifetime?

7. **April 3**

Have your roles each been distinct, or are there commonalities threaded between each of them?

8. **April 4**

How do you play your roles? With a firm upper hand or with compassion?

9. **April 5**

As you have matured, has the way you have played your roles changed at all?

10. **April 6**

How have you played roles usually reserved for later in life (caregiver, retiree) or ones from earlier in life (child, one who is cared for)?

11. **April 7**

If souls do not play roles but serve a function, who in your current lifetime do you feel is operating with a dominant soul?

12. **April 8**

What influence have soul-dominant individuals had throughout your current lifetime?

13. ## April 9

What percentage of relationships in your current lifetime do you feel involved characters who were strictly role-playing?

14. ## April 10

Were these relationships from April 9 easy or difficult to maintain?

15. ## April 11

If you look back at favorite characters from your current lifetime, would they be classified as role-players or free spirits?

16. ## April 12

If a free spirit is defined as someone who cannot be defined, how do you feel they function in a world that expects role-playing?

17. ## April 13

What expectations do you have for yourself in regard to how you play various roles that have been assigned to you?

18. ## April 14

Are you aware of any expectations that people who interact with you have about the roles you play?

19. ## April 15

Is it important for you to feel as if you are meeting explicitly stated expectations for your role-playing?

20. ## April 16

Is it important for you to feel as if you are meeting implied expectations for your role-playing?

21. **April 17**

How do you feel when others express feeling let down by your role-playing performance(s)?

22. **April 18**

Reflect on a recent time when you felt that you were not living up to your potential.

23. **April 19**

Do you understand that the phrase used in April 18 – "living up to your potential" – refers to external or internalized role-playing expectations?

24. **April 20**

If all role-playing and all external and internalized expectations for role-playing come from the ego, would it be possible for you to allow unconditional love to fuel how you play your roles?

25. **April 21**

What fears do you have about playing your roles with less fear and rigidity and more love and openness?

26. **April 22**

Reflect on a recent time when you encountered someone who was in a role but played it with compassion and understanding.

27. **April 23**

Reflect on a recent time when you yourself played a role with compassion and understanding.

28. April 24

Describe your own role-playing in a recent relationship that you consider to be closely personal and emotionally intimate.

29. April 25

Moving forward, can you commit to using less rigidity in your relationships?

30. April 26

Moving forward, can you commit to using more fluidity before deciding what to do or say in your relationships?

31. April 27

Can you understand that role-playing is rooted in the past and is not centered in *Now* time – the only time there is?

32. April 28

Are you willing to risk having your relationships change if you move away from role-playing?

33. April 29

Are you willing to experience more freedom and less stress if you shift from fear to love?

34. April 30

Can you let go of your attachments to role-playing in order to become a more soul-driven character?

May: Character Assassination

1. The mind wants to classify everything in terms that it can understand. Good and bad are the most basic categories, and all the others stem from that. The mind prefers not to think of itself as bad but will do so in its attempt at fairness. The first target for being categorized as bad is other people. They are bad if they have broken any of the innumerable rules a particular mind subscribes to. If they break these rules or don't subscribe to them to begin with, then they are bad or evil themselves. This is character assassination. One false move and you're dead, so to speak. Characters are branded with the scarlet letter *B* if they say or do something that is out of step with a singular or collective entity. This can range from breaking a posted rule or mandated law to merely offending the evaluator and everything in between.

2. Both groups and individuals make decisions to exclude others for various violations of ethics or behavior. These can be preemptive strikes to prevent a relationship from even starting with the offending party. This can also happen at any time during a relationship, which can become severely strained or permanently severed. The young and old alike have dead bodies of assassinated characters surrounding them. The lucky have managed to keep them in the past, but many are haunted by these ghosts who are known as shadow figures.

3. The mind becomes angry about nearly everything under the sun that is not the way it thinks it should be. Then it blames everyone near and far for their possible involvement. Characters carry all of this around

with them from one day to the next, one year to the next, and one decade to the next. Blame and shame take their toll on a character's health and happiness. If you create your life through reactions (fear) at times and responses (love) at other times, you can see the obvious effects and tolls that they take. Characters receive projected "shame on yous" and somewhere along the line start to believe them. There aren't many characters who don't blame themselves and others for why things didn't happen the way their mind's thoughts said they should have happened.

4. **Guidelines**: Pick a time of day that suits you best and read the step that corresponds to the appropriate month and date. This is your starting point. Simply reflect on what the step means to you and ways to put it into practice. Accept whatever feelings come to the surface as you work your way through the steps. These steps are the beginning of a transformation where love replaces fear, which is no easy feat. Be patient with yourself. You are doing what few have ever been able to do. Now you have the means. Just add a little willingness and you will be a more soulful and less ego-driven being in just a year's time. Godspeed.

5. May 1

Character assassination starts with thoughts, so let's start there and let's stay close to home. How have you blamed yourself for something that happened recently?

6. May 2

What things from the past do you still blame yourself for?

7. May 3

If you are aware of these, and only if you were explicitly told about them, what things do others currently blame you for?

8. **May 4**

If you are aware of these, and only if you were explicitly told about them, what characters from your past blamed you for things that did not go the way they wanted?

9. **May 5**

How has your own character assassination interfered in your relationships?

10. **May 6**

If gossip is defined as a verbal conversation between two or more people who are involved in blaming others about things they may or may not have been involved in, when was the last time you participated in this?

11. **May 7**

If you refused to gossip, what might happen to your relationship with others in the group?

12. **May 8**

Have you ever walked away from an interaction that involved gossip? What consequences did you face?

13. **May 9**

Can being called a "goody two shoes" or someone who is "holier than thou" be another type of character assassination?

14. **May 10**

When was the most recent time you assassinated a character you know personally?

15. May 11

For the May 10 exercise, were the things you said confirmable, factual data? Or were they things you heard that you were passing on?

16. May 12

Staying with this same incident, what was your motivation for assassinating someone's character?

17. May 13

If someone makes a choice that you would not have made, is this something that truly warrants any type of criticism?

18. May 14

How do you feel when your choices in life are subject to criticism?

19. May 15

Is any criticism ever warranted?

20. May 16

If criticism is sometimes warranted, who is it that is the standard bearer?

21. May 17

If criticism is sometimes warranted, who is it that is the enforcer of the standard(s)?

22. May 18

If you were to speculate, how much of character assassination is steeped in the desire to control others?

23. **May 19**

What would it take for you to become that person who finally admits "who am I to talk"?

24. **May 20**

Is character assassination life affirming and supportive of others?

25. **May 21**

Is character assassination respectful or disrespectful?

26. **May 22**

Is it okay for anyone to criticize public figures?

27. **May 23**

Do you ever say things online that you would never say in person?

28. **May 24**

Is it okay for someone to be made fun of if it is done in a joking type of way?

29. **May 25**

Every character assassination has a cumulative effect. Each one cuts like a knife. Can you pledge to stop criticizing yourself and harming yourself in the process?

30. **May 26**

Can you pledge to reconsider the harmful effects of criticism and not excuse them as "just part of life, we all have to grow a thick skin"?

31. **May 27**

Character assassination is a specific type of bullying. Can you pledge to build people up and not tear them down?

32. **May 28**

Is it okay with you that many comedians target people in the audience or well-known people for put-downs at their expense?

33. **May 29**

If you stop quietly condoning this behavior and let it be known that you will no longer tolerate it, you may lose friends but can make new ones of a higher quality. Are you ready to move away from character assassination?

34. **May 30**

There is a belief that children can be quite cruel, and this has circulated through the collective for decades. What can adults do to promote more soulful behavior in children?

35. **May 31**

What is your takeaway from the May reflections on character assassination?

June: Feelings

1. The biggest complication about being human is that humans have both thoughts and feelings. Many of these feelings are connected to the thoughts. An example is a fire or flood that caused all of the property belonging to the character and their family to be destroyed. The house is no longer habitable. Personal treasures are gone. Family heirlooms are gone. All of the things one needs in this world, such as clothing, appliances, furniture, or a vehicle of some type are no longer there. They have been reduced to ash or unusable junk. How would a directly impacted human feel about something as life altering as this? The feelings may fluctuate between intense sadness, a feeling of desperation and hopelessness, fear about what to do next, and intense anger at life or God. They may say, "Why did this have to happen to me?"

2. In situations like these, the biggest obstacle to acceptance and peace is the character's attachments to the home and its contents. The character felt secure in this home, surrounded by these now destroyed belongings. The idea of security has given the house and pieces of property additional meaning. The idea that "these are mine" has meant something to the character. And when there isn't anything left, what does it mean then? Where will they sleep and what will they wear? Will they be homeless and, if so, what would this mean for the involved character? In this scenario that happens in real life all too frequently, the character's thoughts and feelings become one big, jumbled-up mess. What to do? How can you more easily separate the two?

3. Now you've finally discovered what was truly meant in the original

A Course in Miracles when the term *insane* was used to describe humans. It isn't because I was talking trash about them, it's because being human is so confusing. Even those who aren't dealing with a major stressor like losing a home to a fire or flood, are in some state of confusion most all of the time about whatever they might be going through. They have to sort through the tangled-up web of thoughts and feelings and attempt to function in this world at the same time. My hat's off to each of you. But how can more soul presence help to sort thoughts from feelings?

4. More soul presence is the primary purpose of this new version of an old book. We want to promote peace and love with less ego, less fear, more soul, and more love. This may sound impossible in today's crazy world, but this is the only hope here. Your soul will help you to process all of your feelings, but the one thing it can't do, the one thing it isn't allowed to do, is to interfere with and control your thoughts. The first step in any ordinary or extraordinary situation you may be involved in is to clear out your incessant thoughts, so that you can process your feelings. And this can't happen right away after a large amount of stress. Give it time. Be patient. And when you're ready, ask "What would love have me do in this situation? Who does it want me to talk to and what should I say?"

5. **Guidelines**: Pick a time of day that suits you best and read the step that corresponds to the appropriate month and date. This is your starting point. Simply reflect on what the step means to you and ways to put it into practice. Accept whatever feelings come to the surface as you work your way through the steps. These steps are the beginning of a transformation where love replaces fear, which is no easy feat. Be patient with yourself. You are doing what few have ever been able to do. Now you have the means. Just add a little willingness and you will be a more soulful and less ego-driven being in just a year's time. Godspeed.

6. June 1

Which feeling or set of feelings do you find to be the most difficult to deal with?

7. June 2

Do you have negative thoughts about your feelings, such as ones that say you shouldn't have certain feelings?

8. June 3

Can you see that moving towards acceptance of your feelings will help you move away from conflict with them?

9. June 4

Give an example of a recent time when you judged your feelings as bad, and you felt as if you were a bad person for having them.

10. June 5

Give an example of a time when you talked about a situation and your feelings about this situation with a friend or family member, and you walked away feeling ashamed.

11. June 6

Have you ever knowingly or unknowingly shamed someone in an effort to help them by controlling them?

12. June 7

Between thoughts and feelings, which ones may be more trustworthy in the sense that they can lead to a greater level of understanding and peace?

13. June 8

Give an example when information you discovered later wasn't true, and it produced strong, reactive feelings.

14. June 9

Give an example when a feeling prompted you to use your mind to obtain factual information about a situation.

15. June 10

Do you use your mind or does your mind use you?

16. June 11

Can you make time on a daily basis to sort through your thoughts and feelings and find the true feelings that are not just reactions to thoughts?

17. June 12

Can you be compassionate towards others without feeling so bad about their situation that you lose your own sense of peace?

18. June 13

Unhappy thoughts lead to unhappiness. True or false?

19. June 14

Happy thoughts lead to happiness. True or false?

20. June 15

All feelings come from your soul, but the loving, positive ones that are not instigated by thoughts are considered true feelings. All other feelings are considered transitory ones that lead to truth once properly processed.

21. June 16

Feelings that originate from love need to be discerned from feelings that lead to love.

22. June 17

You cannot master your feelings, but you can allow your feelings to master you when you are ready.

23. June 18

Reflect on a time when you made a decision not to do something. For example, not take a new job that ended up being the correct decision because you made it based on your gut instincts.

24. June 19

Anger is a potent feeling. It originates with thoughts about the unfairness of actions and situations. Moving forward, when I feel angry I will make it my habit to sit with it until I am ready to release it.

25. June 20

A planned release of anger, so that love can replace it, includes things such as remediation. Oftentimes others do need to hear how their actions have impacted you in negative ways.

26. June 21

Love includes all feelings, like an envelope has space for a letter or card. My job is to love all of my feelings.

27. June 22

Because some of my feelings may come from inaccurate information or misinformation from someone who may have wanted to deceive me, I am always willing to apologize to anyone that my feelings mislead me about.

28. June 23

Because the ego isn't always forthcoming, I will make it my habit, moving forward, to listen to the deeper content and not just the surface words. This will help with processing my own feelings.

29. June 24

Moving forward, I will listen to my own words and will dig deeper to discover my own true feelings about any subject.

30. June 25

What are ways I like to use to release my own pent-up feelings?

31. June 26

I refuse to beat myself up for having this feeling or that feeling.

32. June 27

I accept that my feelings make me, me.

33. June 28

I am a beautiful, feeling character and soul.

34. June 29

If someone would like to process their thoughts and feelings with me, I will be honest in setting up boundaries about whether this would be a healthy activity for me or not.

35. June 30

I cannot allow anyone to use me as they see fit. I will decide my role in any relationship based on my comfort level, which will always be based on my feelings.

July: The Holy Instant

1. If human thoughts and feelings create an insane, jumbled-up mess, then the Holy Instant is time of sanity. It is time outside of time when a character acknowledges the soul and the soul's connection to the all of all. It is timeless time of no thoughts, no concerns, and no worries. It has no past and no future. It is where the soul's power lives. It is not part of the human world and experience, as it is outside of them. It is reality, outside of a world of illusion.

2. Anytime you want to leave this world experience, you can. You are wearing your ruby slippers, but instead of saying, "I wish I was in Kansas" simply say, "I Am here in this place now, where I Am to learn more about my soul, and in doing so allow it to grow and transform everything within and without." As the inside changes, the perspective changes. Me becomes we. Selfishness becomes selflessness. The Holy Instant is a reminder of your true identity, and it is available to all, at all times. No concussion required.

3. The Holy Instant is a thoughtless state of mindlessness and soulfulness. It is a reminder that you are not who you think you are, but are one of divine essence, a soul connected to all other souls, the totality of which creates God, the source energy that created everything you know about

and everything you do not. It is as mysterious as the real you is, undefined and formless, informed by the all of all. Give it a spin. Picture yourself in stillness, consumed by light, and explore. What do you discover? Stay awhile and return often. You will never be the same again. You are a portal into the unknown, where the unknown can become known through you. This is reality. This is your reality.

4. **Guidelines**: Pick a time of day that suits you best and read the step that corresponds to the appropriate month and date. This is your starting point. Simply reflect on what the step means to you and ways to put it into practice. Accept whatever feelings come to the surface as you work your way through the steps. These steps are the beginning of a transformation where love replaces fear, which is no easy feat. Be patient with yourself. You are doing what few have ever been able to do. Now you have the means. Just add a little willingness and you will be a more soulful and less ego-driven being in just a year's time. Godspeed.

5. July 1

What are your initial responses to learning about the Holy Instant?

6. July 2

The Holy Instant repairs the rift between the wholeness of the soul and the fractured reality of the human character.

7. July 3

Timelessness and mindlessness call to you through the Holy Instant.

8. July 4

As unreal as the Holy Instant seems, it is reality that regular human life lacks.

9. July 5

Each time you exit the Holy Instant, your soul has become charged up and is stronger as a result.

10. July 6

What are your experiences from your initial tries at the Holy Instant?

11. July 7

As you have discovered more about your true identity, what feelings have surfaced?

12. July 8

My true identity is reinforced during the Holy Instant.

13. July 9

My true identity is something that can assist me in processing everyday life.

14. July 10

My true identity of soul is like an invaluable jewel.

15. July 11

All hope and trust comes from my soul.

16. July 12

The Holy Instant is like a wonderful drug without any side effects.

17. July 13

When faced with any type of decision, small or large, connecting with my soul through the Holy Instant will be beneficial.

18. July 14

My soul can answer any question.

19. July 15

My soul uses love and only unconditional love to express itself.

20. July 16

If my brain gives me a possible solution and my soul also gives me a possible solution, my soul's solution can be counted on as the best one.

21. July 17

My brain is loud, and my soul is quiet. It will take practice to quiet my loud thoughts so that I can hear my soul.

22. July 18

My soul is an aspect of God. I can trust it.

23. July 19

The Holy Instant brings me closer to myself, an aspect of God.

24. July 20

God isn't in some faraway place. God is within all.

25. July 21

I can access God through the Holy Instant.

26. July 22

God hears my prayers when they come from my soul because God can hear itself.

27. July 23

The next time I want to pray to God, I will realize where God is.

28. July 24

God creates by extending itself. It is never separate from its creations.

29. July 25

If you have already experienced your first Holy Instant, how would you describe it in a way that would be encouraging and enthusiastic?

30. July 26

The Holy Instant is the real secret in the world, not the law of attraction, but everyone's true identity as part of God.

31. July 27

No one can save me. I just have to remember my true identity. Then, all doubts and problems will vanish.

32. July 28

The Holy Instant is experienced in the only time there is, which is now.

33. July 29

God lives inside of me.

34. July 30

God looks like me. Humankind was not made in God's image, but God is in the image of every person of every age and gender. God lives next door. God is across the street. God is at the bank and the grocery store. God is rich and God is poor. God is you and God is me. Together we are one.

35. ## July 31

The Holy Instant is a gift to you. It is your birthright. If you only take away one concept from this entire book, let it be this one.

August: Your Relationship with the Unknown

1. All humans are limited to receiving information from their five senses. Occasionally you will come across one or two who are highly intuitive or have a sixth way of obtaining information. Those who use touch, smell, sight, taste, and hearing to gather information may wonder if there is intelligent life in other universes or dimensions. They may wonder what happens to someone who dies. They may wonder about the purpose of life itself and whether or not there is a creator, a devil, heaven, and hell. They may wonder about information contained in religious textbooks and they may wonder about me. Where did I go when I died and where do I live now? What is my purpose in life and do I have a life if I am dead? Where do those who have experienced physical death go and how long do they stay there? What do they do exactly?

2. First of all, I didn't die. No one ever does. It is only the body and the character who are taken out of the play. The souls live on in the formless world, where they live rich, fulfilling lives in service to the God collective. Yes, you will be reunited with your grandparents and your best friend from third grade. You will also be reunited with those who created a great deal of unnecessary stress for you. Everything will be seen clearly for exactly what it was because your blinders will be off. To be human is to be aware of only some things and unaware of most things, so I can

compare it to being blind. Humans only see bits and pieces and not the whole picture. They don't get the opportunity to see how everything connects. This is a symptom of the illusionary cause of being a human.

3. Have you been interested in ghosts or UFOs? Many are afraid of things that are outside of their familiarity and comfort zone, but do they have to be? Many have wrongly been taught that believing in these things or investigating them by reading books or conducting research is evil and is from a devil of some type. What if I told you that there are spirit beings roaming the earth? What if I told you that there could be several sharing the same space you are in now? You are in a dimension of time and space, and you believe that there is space between where you are sitting and the big screen TV. But what if I told you that the space you think is there is actually a dimension that is occupied by other types of beings, ones who aren't aliens but who are very much a part of us and of God? This is the reality of the situation.

4. **Guidelines**: Pick a time of day that suits you best and read the step that corresponds to the appropriate month and date. This is your starting point. Simply reflect on what the step means to you and ways to put it into practice. Accept whatever feelings come to the surface as you work your way through the steps. These steps are the beginning of a transformation where love replaces fear, which is no easy feat. Be patient with yourself. You are doing what few have ever been able to do. Now you have the means. Just add a little willingness and you will be a more soulful and less ego-driven being in just a year's time. Godspeed.

5. August 1

Think back to a time when you equated the unseen with monsters who wanted to harm you. Did it keep this subject in the dark for you as you grew into adulthood?

6. **August 2**

There is nothing in the unseen world that can harm you.

7. **August 3**

Harmful things are in the world you currently reside in; they are not in the spirit realm.

8. **August 4**

The ego has made sure to keep the spirit realm as a taboo subject. It doesn't want you to know that the spirit realm is your true home.

9. **August 5**

It is the fear of death that keeps the unseen world as a taboo subject.

10. **August 6**

Just as a coin has two sides, so does life.

11. **August 7**

Have you ever felt the presence of a loved one who has passed over to the other side?

12. **August 8**

Have you ever wanted to say something specific to someone who has died?

13. **August 9**

Your words are heard by those you direct them to, whether they have a body or not.

14. ## August 10

Untethered souls communicate through telepathy. When you say something to yourself and direct it towards one of these souls they hear you, as this is the way they communicate also.

15. ## August 11

Traveling through space and time to study other worlds of form has been popular for millennia. It isn't anything to fear.

16. ## August 12

Humans have not yet achieved the level of technology that other civilizations have achieved.

17. ## August 13

The souls you have been closest to in this lifetime are souls you have incarnated with in past lifetimes.

18. ## August 14

Soul companions support and challenge each other.

19. ## August 15

Think of someone you don't like. They are one of your soul companions.

20. ## August 16

Just because a relationship has been difficult or even bad doesn't mean that the involved souls aren't conspiring to bring out the best in their characters.

21. August 17

The next time you are physically alone, without any devices or media of any type, know that you aren't really alone.

22. August 18

The spirit world is as varied and interesting as any physical world.

23. August 19

The job of all in the spirit world is to support all in the spirit world and those in the physical worlds who will let them.

24. August 20

The job of everyone in the physical worlds is to remember their spiritual calling and be of service.

25. August 21

The only law pertaining to both the formless and those animating form is this: do no harm and be helpful.

26. August 22

The law written for August 21 is only broken by those who forget their true identity.

27. August 23

Safety in an unsafe world of form is assured to all of those who act from a place of authenticity.

28. August 24

Knowing you are part of God is what keeps you safe.

29. **August 25**

My role is not to return in form and rule over anyone. My role is to facilitate your awakening and your eventual Christhood.

30. **August 26**

Christ means God in man, God in woman, God in child. Everyone will be Christ when the time is right.

31. **August 27**

A fully dominant and mature soul who has assumed most of the duties of the ego is Christ.

32. **August 28**

Soul-emergent beings are part of God too, but their functionality and power are not at the consistently high level of Christ.

33. **August 29**

All of creation will help you question your ego's beliefs, so that you can listen to and express from your soul more often.

34. **August 30**

Your spirit helpers cannot help you unless you explicitly ask for their help and grant them permission.

35. **August 31**

I live in the spirit world and in the physical world. I never really left my true home.

September: Love

1. Have you ever fallen in love and then fallen out of it? These strong feelings that attracted you to someone in the first place may have seemed like love, but the love I Am talking about is very rarely found in the human realm. What is typically found are degrees of like. At the top of this scale is something that mimics love. When it is tested, even severely tested, this almost love quality shows what it is really made out of because it can be withdrawn and dissolved. This can never happen with real, unconditional love. Have a seat and ask yourself if you would still love so and so if they said this or did that? If you reply by saying "yes, but I would have to forgive them first" then I Am here to tell you that this isn't really love, because love never condemns in the first place. Love never needs to forgive.

2. Anything that isn't true unconditional love is a call for love. Who is calling for love? The soul is calling for more of itself, more love energy. The character is not calling for true love because it can't. It doesn't know what true love is. How can it call for something it doesn't even know about and has never experienced? The soul cries for love all over the land. God calls for larger amounts of itself to help counter the effects of a fear-based operating system. These calls have historically gone unanswered because the populace has deliberately been left in the dark about what souls are and how they are the one true identity of everyone.

3. There are those whose love has been tested in the most extreme ways. They have been lied to, physically harmed, stolen from, lied about, and

brought into harm's way by someone, and they still love them. Maybe this person is a blood family member, and they can't cut ties completely. Everyone tries to talk sense into these folks, but they won't listen and the abuse keeps coming. The abuser may call from jail and want money put on a commissary card, and then may assume they have the right to sleep on someone's couch upon release. Maybe they will toe the line for a while, but it won't be long before they fall back into their abusive ways. Is this love? The answer is a firm no. This is an abusive relationship and love cannot, will not, be abused. The abused person in this scenario is being called to love themselves, by refusing to be abused or treated in any way other than stellar. Yes, the abuser is being someone that love cannot be around and cannot tolerate. The abuser's soul is asking for love, but the character is running the show. So the abused person needs to cut their losses and look after their own self, first and foremost. Love says no, softly at times, and firmly at others.

4. **Guidelines**: Pick a time of day that suits you best and read the step that corresponds to the appropriate month and date. This is your starting point. Simply reflect on what the step means to you and ways to put it into practice. Accept whatever feelings come to the surface as you work your way through the steps. These steps are the beginning of a transformation where love replaces fear, which is no easy feat. Be patient with yourself. You are doing what few have ever been able to do. Now you have the means. Just add a little willingness and you will be a more soulful and less ego-driven being in just a year's time. Godspeed.

5. September   1

Give an example of a time when you had to love from a distance for your own well-being.

6. ## September 2

Love is concerned with itself first and foremost.

7. ## September 3

Love extends to love. Souls give love to other souls.

8. ## September 4

The ego is incapable of accepting true love.

9. ## September 5

If someone is accepting true love, this is because their soul is accepting true love and has risen to the surface to do so.

10. ## September 6

Love does not fix anything at the character level. It works from the inside out.

11. ## September 7

No one ever has to do anything to deserve love.

12. ## September 8

All are deserving of love.

13. ## September 9

Love is the only thing here that is real. It is eternal and unchanging.

14. ## September 10

The world is largely an example of the resistance to love.

15. September 11

Love is patient and will wait until someone is ready to receive this gift.

16. September 12

How many times have you fallen in love, only to discover that it wasn't love at all?

17. September 13

It is exciting to apply love or look through its eyes.

18. September 14

Love will show me a whole new world I've never seen before.

19. September 15

When I look through the lens of love, I will see what is love and what is not love.

20. September 16

I'm ready to put aside all of my ideas about love.

21. September 17

My ideas about love come from places where there isn't any love.

22. September 18

Movies, TV shows, social media, romance novels, and my own character's experiences don't really explain what love is, although they all purport to do so.

23. September 19

The only thing that truly knows love is itself.

24. September 20

My soul is love.

25. September 21

I can trust what my soul shows me as I open up to it.

26. September 22

I am willing to put aside what I think love is, so I can discover what it really is.

27. September 23

Do I think unconditional love may be a sign of weakness?

28. September 24

Am I afraid to live in such a violent world with love as my guide?

29. September 25

Love is unrestricted care and concern for oneself and for others.

30. September 26

Love embraces both itself and everything that isn't love yet.

31. September 27

Love accepts the absence of love as a challenge. The whole reason we are all here is to simply shine light on the absence of love.

32. September 28

Love doesn't judge or attack anything. Judgment and attack are in the realm of ego, not soul.

33. September 29

Love makes decisions on what is love and what is not love yet.

34. September 30

When you wake up each morning ask this question: "what will love have me do today, or does it want me to be still and simply be?"

October: Grief

1. If all things in life are potential lessons where an individual can choose love over fear, then the processing of grief, the pain felt over loss, is by far the greatest lesson with the greatest possible rewards. The two key words in the previous sentence are *potential* and *possible*. Grief's potential is often sidelined, as the pain caused by not understanding the hard things in life takes center stage. Grief can be carried throughout an entire lifetime. It can be added to. It can double, triple, and finally consume a precious lifetime. Its self-blame component can produce devastating disease that shortens a life span. It is the cause of many suicides and other types of self-destructive behavior. Some grief takes an outward form and creates events that harm or even take the lives of others.

2. Grief is an example of a time when the illusionary human identity

produces something so devastating that it can threaten a soul's entire human lifetime. Grief does not exist in the spirit world as there is no loss in love. However, grief is a very real part of this alternative reality. I don't want to say something broad like "it's all an illusion" and make light of all the very serious situations here in what is your reality. You and every single reader's reality is being human. It is very different from the reality you came from, but it is the reality you are in. Therefore, things like grief are very real for you, and I want to help you look at it through the eyes of love, with a fresh perspective. It would be nice if you could just wish it away, wouldn't it? Wishing something would go away isn't practical, and it isn't what love wants either. Your soul wants you to understand everything in a real way, in a loving way, in a healthy way.

3. Grief is the trickiest of feelings because it is identity mixed with loss, mixed with a flood of thoughts that are all connected. "I feel terrible that this happened." "What will I do now that I have lost this person or this situation?" "Could I have done more?" "Could I have done anything differently?" "Am I to blame for this?" Psychologists have correctly identified grief as having stages. The problem is that there isn't any guarantee that the stages will flow into each other. A person can get stuck in one of the stages and resist movement and healing. Grief has been very accurately described as a stab in the gut. It physically hurts, and this hurt can last a long time or the rest of someone's life. What does love have to say about this? Remembering your true identity will certainly help. While in the Holy Instant, ask your soul what you should do moment to moment. It will remind you not to pretend that you aren't human. Feel what you're feeling and allow the process to take as long as it needs to take. The purpose of this book is to remind you that you aren't wholly human. You are both human and divine, so please honor both, for your own sake.

4. **Guidelines**: Pick a time of day that suits you best and read the step that corresponds to the appropriate month and date. This is your starting point. Simply reflect on what the step means to you and ways to put it into practice. Accept whatever feelings come to the surface as you work your way through the steps. These steps are the beginning of a transformation where love replaces fear, which is no easy feat. Be patient with yourself. You are doing what few have ever been able to do. Now you have the means. Just add a little willingness and you will be a more soulful and less ego-driven being in just a year's time. Godspeed.

5. October 1

Grief arrives when trauma is unresolved.

6. October 2

Revisit a time of grief in your life experience. Were you able to be patient and loving with yourself during this time?

7. October 3

Is there accumulated grief that you carry around from things that you are unable to release?

8. October 4

Have you met anyone who was unpleasant and hard to get along with? If so, realize that there is trauma and grief there.

9. October 5

Returning to the October 2 exercise, which people helped you during this time period?

10. October 6

Returning to the October 2 exercise, which things helped you during this time period?

11. October 7

It can be a long road from grief to acceptance, but once you are there healing is complete.

12. October 8

Death is commonly thought of when the topic of grief is brought up. Does knowing the role death plays in the physical world help you with this concept?

13. October 9

What other issues in your life experience produced trauma that triggered grief?

14. October 10

Learning to prevent trauma is a healthy way to avoid grief.

15. October 11

Practicing the Holy Instant and sorting through your feelings about hard things that happen in the physical world is one way to keep your feelings from solidifying.

16. October 12

Practicing complete forgiveness for those who have angered or disappointed you is another way to release feelings before grief sets in or even after it sets in.

17. ## October 13

Ideas that become attached to events and situations invite grief.

18. ## October 14

One idea that invites grief is "that should not have happened."

19. ## October 15

One idea that invites grief is "if only."

20. ## October 16

One idea that invites grief is "I should have."

21. ## October 17

Upon the death of a loved one, missing their physical presence is part of being human.

22. ## October 18

Upon the death of a loved one, missing the conversations you used to share is part of being human.

23. ## October 19

Upon the death of a loved one, missing shared activities is part of being human.

24. ## October 20

Oftentimes, the death of a family member may suddenly cast you into a new and different role in the family.

25. October 21

Oftentimes, death brings survivor's guilt to those who have been left behind.

26. October 22

Oftentimes, conflict pays an unwelcome visit following the death of a family member.

27. October 23

I can infuse any situation surrounding the death of a loved one with love from my soul.

28. October 24

My soul can guide me to make any situation involving a death at least a little better.

29. October 25

The physical and emotional pain from grief can last a lifetime.

30. October 26

The physical and emotional pain from grief can be temporary if I allow love to show me the way out.

31. October 27

The physical and emotional pain from grief can be overcome with love as my guide.

32. October 28

The physical and emotional pain from grief can be transformative if I allow it and do not resist it.

33. October 29

Grief can be my teacher.

34. October 30

Grief can teach me to love the parts of me where I hurt.

35. October 31

Grief and the pain it causes may be the hardest lesson for me while I am on the earth.

November: Acceptance

1. It is easy to accept things you like, but things you don't ... not so much. Living a life of acceptance simply means that you acknowledge that there is very little in your control. You watch it all happen as the observer. You observe what others have chosen to make observable: the good, the bad, and the ugly. You do it without being emotionally invested, without losing your neutrality. Easier said than done. As a feeling, sentient being, you feel angry or sad at what you see. You want to help those involved, but too much emotional involvement on your part could end up hurting you by robbing you of your peace and disconnecting you from your soul's feelings of love. How can you accept all that goes on in the world without feeling somehow drawn into it?

2. When you identify more as soul, you start to disempower things and events and see them as what they are. Everything can happen here, from the most loving and joyous to the most dastardly. You have to

take the good with the bad and somehow come out clean in the wash. The negative things, the bad things, are as much a part of life here as the positive ones are. But how can you understand life's dark side, what we refer to as the resistance to love? I say stop trying. Stop giving yourself headaches and stomachaches by trying to figure out why this happened or why that happened and just try to accept that it happened. Look at the facts, accept them, and move on. Not to be cavalier about it, but try to limit the power some of life's horrors have over you. They were difficult enough to begin with without giving them permission to hurt you.

3. Acceptance doesn't mean fighting. It is not opposition to anything. It isn't a hard-liner's staunch stance. Accept that you don't like it. Accept that it is happening even though you don't want it to. Accept that you think it is fair, but someone else is in opposition to what you think. Accept that change is inevitable, and that something positive may rise from the ashes. Acceptance doesn't mean you don't have values and don't care about anything. It means that you understand that much of life is outside your realm of control. If you do have control over some things, then value those things, and allow your soul to use its voice to infuse unconditional love into any situation.

4. **Guidelines**: Pick a time of day that suits you best and read the step that corresponds to the appropriate month and date. This is your starting point. Simply reflect on what the step means to you and ways to put it into practice. Accept whatever feelings come to the surface as you work your way through the steps. These steps are the beginning of a transformation where love replaces fear, which is no easy feat. Be patient with yourself. You are doing what few have ever been able to do. Now you have the means. Just add a little willingness and you will be a more soulful and less ego-driven being in just a year's time. Godspeed.

5. November 1

What have you never accepted one hundred percent?

6. November 2

Can you see from the November 1 exercise that the lack of acceptance in this case has brought you pain?

7. November 3

Blame prevents acceptance.

8. November 4

Who do you blame for your response to the November 1 prompt? Yourself or someone else?

9. November 5

Use this day to reflect throughout your current life experience to discover other things or situations that you have never fully accepted.

10. November 6

The opposite of to accept is to reject.

11. November 7

Which things or situations did you finally accept and come to peace about in your current lifetime experience?

12. November 8

Have you ever been rejected by a potential friend because of something they heard about you?

13. November 9

Have you ever rejected a potential friendship because of something you heard about them?

14. November 10

Have you ever rejected a potential friendship for fear about what others would say if they saw you with the person in question?

15. November 11

Have you ever been rejected as a potential friend by someone who did not want to be seen with you?

16. November 12

Reflect on an established relationship that you ended because you did not accept something you had recently discovered about them.

17. November 13

Growing up, did you feel like you had to behave in certain ways, or be a certain way, in order to be accepted?

18. November 14

Being acceptable is a list of arbitrary standards that indicate conditional acceptance.

19. November 15

Conditional acceptance is not true acceptance.

20. November 16

"No shirt, no shoes, no service" is not true acceptance.

21. November 17

Dress codes are not true acceptance.

22. November 18

If you have been a parent, or even a childcare provider at any point in your current lifetime, did you promote the message that the children had to conform by jumping through hoops in order to be accepted?

23. November 19

In order to stay out of society's conflicts, can you accept that you feel strongly about certain things and others do not feel the same way about them?

24. November 20

Agreeing to disagree is a form of acceptance of inevitable differences of opinion.

25. November 21

I accept that I am not my thoughts.

26. November 22

I accept that I am not who I have always thought I was.

27. November 23

I accept that I'm not only who I thought I was, but am also soul, a part of God.

28. November 24

The love of God will help me accept things and people I have rejected.

29. November 25

Rejection is not love.

30. November 26

Accepting others for who they are doesn't mean that it is in my best interests to be around them.

31. November 27

I accept that others may be strongly resisting love and that it may be difficult to be around them.

32. November 28

I can bless everyone and not curse anyone.

33. November 29

I accept that like attracts like and things that are dissimilar may not mutually benefit from each other's company.

34. November 30

I accept that I can save no one. They must save themselves from themselves.

December: Forgiveness

1. Forgiveness was a major theme in the original *A Course in Miracles*. In this book we explore all of the things that can lead to the miracle of

forgiveness and all of the miracles that can prevent the need for forgiveness in the first place. In this world, in the kingdom of the ego, forgiveness is a necessary tool for self-preservation. In the spirit realm, where souls roam, there is no forgiveness because there is no condemnation. Forgiveness is the shedding of a false idea. It is usually about others but can be about oneself too. Forgiveness means that an individual has no need or right to condemn. Condemning makes them a liar against God itself because they are saying that God's process for growing and changing is invalid.

2. Forgiveness is the final step towards authenticity or truth telling. In the world of the ego there is no truth, only small degrees of it. Remember that the standard for truth is one hundred percent true, one hundred percent of the time. What does forgiveness lead to? It leads to freedom because lies and lying are tyrannical. There is no freedom in tyranny. And there is no freedom in the world of ego, which is, by its nature, a place by and for slaves. Both the slave and the slave master are controlled, and this control prevents freedom and the vision that accompanies it.

3. Forgiveness releases guilt. Without forgiveness, guilt will wreak havoc. Take a look around the world to see what guilt has brought to Mother Gaia. Even the guiltless that roam the streets looking for their next victim, for their next drug fix, feel guilt if even for fleeting seconds. Forgiveness is part and parcel of freedom, and freedom is what is required for a soul-based experience in any world of form, especially this one.

4. **Guidelines**: Pick a time of day that suits you best and read the step that corresponds to the appropriate month and date. This is your starting point. Simply reflect on what the step means to you and ways to put it into practice. Accept whatever feelings come to the surface as you work your way through the steps. These steps are the beginning of a transformation where love replaces fear, which is no easy feat. Be patient

with yourself. You are doing what few have ever been able to do. Now you have the means. Just add a little willingness and you will be a more soulful and less ego-driven being in just a year's time. Godspeed.

5. December   1

Who have you had to forgive multiple times?

6. December   2

Have you been forgiven multiple times by the same person?

7. December   3

Forgiven means overlooked. The slate is wiped clean.

8. December   4

Forgiveness is required for my own peace of mind.

9. December   5

Part of acceptance is that my role in judgment of a situation has made the situation worse.

10. December   6

Accepting more equals judging less.

11. December   7

When I forgive, I give a gift to myself.

12. December   8

I don't need to be forgiven for my sake but for yours.

13. December 9

When I forgive, I start with myself.

14. December 10

I forgive myself for all of the times I believed I fell short.

15. December 11

I forgive myself for any and all harm I may have caused anyone.

16. December 12

I forgive all who either intentionally or unintentionally caused harm to me.

17. December 13

I forgive life for not always delivering the goods I have wanted.

18. December 14

I forgive all others who had it easier than I did.

19. December 15

I forgive all others who had more than I did.

20. December 16

I forgive all others who had less than I did.

21. December 17

I forgive all others who had it harder than me.

22. December 18

I forgive myself for thinking that I know all the facts necessary to judge anyone about anything.

23. December 19

Forgiveness is the key to my happiness now.

24. December 20

My future nows depend on me being free from the past.

25. December 21

This afternoon I can choose to forgive and release the morning.

26. December 22

Without forgiveness my own behavior and judgments are like a chain around my neck.

27. December 23

Without forgiveness the behavior and words emanating from others are like a ball and chain around my ankles.

28. December 24

Forgiveness is the best gift I can give myself.

29. December 25

Forgiveness is the best gift anyone can give themselves.

30. December 26

I know that I cannot rush forgiveness.

31. December 27

Forgiveness needs time to develop and flower.

32. December 28

As I replace a curse with a blessing, I will need to go through the forgiveness process less often.

33. December 29

Without forgiveness my judgments are capable of great harm to myself.

34. December 30

Without forgiveness my judgments are capable of great harm to others.

35. December 31

While I cannot control much of what life shows me, I can control my reactions through forgiveness.

Epilogue

1. Whether you took an entire year to complete the "Steps to Authenticity" or discovered a meaningful way to think about them with your brain and feel them with your soul's heart, the question now is twofold: "What just happened?" and "What's next?"

2. What just happened is that you were able to dig deeply underneath

the programmed and conditioned mind to give your soul an opportunity to speak, maybe for the first significant time. It has a lot to say but is usually prevented from saying it. Now you know it is there and you know how to access it. You know the importance of each month's topic.

3. What's next? Next, I would like for you to lead or show the way by example. The former *Manual for Teachers* in the original course will now be known in this new book as "The Gift of Wisdom." It will be geared towards sharing what you know and supporting emerging souls in the world. This will also be a twelve-month program but with a twist. Let us begin.

Chapter Eight

The Gift of Wisdom

Introduction

1. "The Gift of Wisdom" is the name of what was formerly known as the *Manual for Teachers*. It comprises twelve sections, one for each month of the year, each addressing one of the twelve strands of wisdom. Like the "Steps to Authenticity" in Chapter Seven, it has an entry for each day of the year, including a leap year entry. The premise for this chapter is that readers have opened up to the idea of living a soul-based life by going through the "Steps to Authenticity" and are ready to live this type of life by lighting the way for others. What is the twist I referred to in the epilogue of "Steps to Authenticity"?

2. The twist is that your soul, or God, will be talking directly to you as you. It will inform your body's brain about love's approach in the form of daily affirmations geared towards specific subject matter. It is one thing to know you have a soul, but it is another one entirely to know that you are one.

January: Patience

1. The ego wants what the ego wants when the ego wants it. The soul, however, is patient and allows things to unfold as they may. The ego wants to explore what life has to offer, but the soul allows life to explore and unfold as it wills to do so, without interruption or resistance. Patience is a virtue for both soul-emergent characters and soul-dominant characters. They both benefit from allowing this soul quality to enhance their life experiences. What does your soul have to say about patience? Let it speak. Let it remind you. Quiet the mind long enough to hear its guidance.

2. What is the opposite of patience? Impatience, which says I want this now or I need this to happen now. It is focused on speeding up future outcomes and bringing them into the now dimension of time. Patience accepts whatever is already here now and enjoys that. It can enjoy empty space before the new family moves in. It enjoys the quiet and doesn't need background noise. It enjoys being with those it is with and isn't focused on those who aren't coming. Patience accepts wanting but can put it off and wait for it. Patience enjoys anticipation. Patience is never in a hurry because its time is already here. It is now.

3. **Guidelines**: Readers should delve directly into "The Gift of Wisdom" after completing all of the "Steps to Authenticity." Simply find the appropriate starting date on the calendar and begin there. Each month of affirmations centers around the theme and each theme is an aspect of wisdom. At the conclusion of this second year, the gift of wisdom will be yours. These exercises will facilitate soul growth by quieting the mind

and retraining it to be in service to the soul and not strictly to the ego. Godspeed to all those who tread these waters to refine their authentic selves into shimmering gems.

4. January 1

I Am is the All of All.

5. January 2

I Am is known as God or source energy.

6. January 3

I Am is your soul in a microcosm state.

7. January 4

I Am is your soul, combined with all souls, combined with the core that never left itself.

8. January 5

I Am explores itself through differentiation.

9. January 6

Soul splitting happens from core energy.

10. January 7

Your soul became "you" for a time.

11. January 8

You don't have a soul; you are a soul.

12. **January 9**

While in the separated state, it seems as though your soul is something other than you.

13. **January 10**

While expanding beyond the separated state, it seems as though your soul is only part of you.

14. **January 11**

When your soul is dominant and mature, you will identify as soul more and more often over time.

15. **January 12**

I Am you and you are I Am.

16. **January 13**

I Am talking to you through your brain.

17. **January 14**

I Am the voice of reason and sanity.

18. **January 15**

You can trust your soul's voice as it only speaks with pure love.

19. **January 16**

The voice you're used to hearing is the voice of me, myself, and I, and it does not speak from pure love.

20. **January 17**

When I speak and you listen, I grow.

21. January 18

When I speak and you choose the voice of ego instead of my voice, I do not grow.

22. January 19

In the separated state, the choice is yours. Choose your true self: the soul and reality. Or choose the false self: the ego and illusion.

23. January 20

I Am is pure patience.

24. January 21

Your soul has been patient while you thought you were someone you're not.

25. January 22

Your soul is you and the character is not you.

26. January 23

The characters you have played have helped you to discover the secret of your true identity.

27. January 24

The characters you have played have pulled you away from unconditional love.

28. January 25

When you choose unconditional love and service, you have the character apparatus to thank.

29. January 26

Something always seems amiss with the character-mind-body apparatus.

30. January 27

You are not the roles you play.

31. January 28

When you play your roles as soul, love will be your guide.

32. January 29

When you play your roles as pure ego, fear will be your guide.

33. January 30

You are love and exceedingly patient.

34. January 31

I Am your voice now.

February: Consideration For The Body

1. The body is said to be a temple. I would add that it is not to be an empty shell whose only purpose is to be a temple for the ego's whims and desires. It is a temple for the soul. Therefore, the body's purpose is ultimately to be the home for God. God goes by many different names. God can be called Jesus, Mary, Elizabeth, or Juan. Each soul or

microcosm of God is at least somewhat different from one another, and some are extraordinarily different. God has an unlimited amount of names and can express in an unlimited amount of ways. The body allows expression from both the ego and the soul. Expression from pure ego shortens the lifespan of the body, and expression from a mixture of both leads to longer longevity. Pure soul expression is rare. This has the longest longevity because soul is much easier on the body and not at all harsh, like the ego often is.

2. What is the body for? It facilitates and enables the growth of God. God grows and develops when it is able to express love through the body or mind-body vehicle. The body's natural operating system is fear, and fear is closed to unconditional love. When life challenges fear to open up to another way, love can begin to speak. Maybe a word here. Maybe a sentence there. As hard as life here on earth is, this is ultimately what is going on within every single body, of every age, of every gender expression. They are all ultimately doing only one thing, even though it looks like they are doing billions of different things simultaneously. They are answering the only true question that there is. Will I choose fear, or will I choose love, with what life has laid out before me?

3. **Guidelines**: Readers should delve directly into the "Gift of Wisdom" after completing all of the "Steps to Authenticity." Simply find the appropriate starting date on the calendar and begin there. Each month of affirmations centers around the theme and each theme is an aspect of wisdom. At the conclusion of this second year, the gift of wisdom will be yours. These exercises will facilitate soul growth by quieting the mind and retraining it to be in service to the soul and not strictly to the ego. Godspeed to all those who tread these waters to refine their authentic selves into shimmering gems.

4. February 1

I Am seeks to express itself through the body.

5. February 2

How I Am expresses varies from body to body.

6. February 3

Characteristics like personality and temperament, as well as aptitude, affect how I Am manifests in different bodies.

7. February 4

I Am you, the real you.

8. February 5

I Am responds with love through the body.

9. February 6

The ego reacts with fear through the body.

10. February 7

The body makes me feel separate and alone or united and together with other bodies.

11. February 8

Having the experience of being a character with a body is designed to help me find my true identity.

12. February 9

The body has helped my soul to hide outside of you.

13. February 10

God is not outside of the body. God activates the body and waits for acknowledgement.

14. February 11

I Am will tell you what your body needs in terms of food and exercise.

15. February 12

I Am will prompt you to move or feed your body, if you allow it to do so.

16. February 13

I Am may agree with secular advice about the body's needs at times.

17. February 14

I Am may disagree with secular advice about the body's needs at times.

18. February 15

Listening to your body means listening to I Am.

19. February 16

I Am activates the body and knows how to care for it.

20. February 17

There are times when I Am may prompt you to obtain medical advice and care.

21. **February 18**

There are times when I Am may ask for space to conduct its own evaluation before any action on your part is requested.

22. **February 19**

Things like vaccinations help to prevent the spread of disease in the populace.

23. **February 20**

While you are here and have an emerging soul, you are very susceptible to contagious disease.

24. **February 21**

While you are here and have a dominant soul, you are less susceptible to contagious disease.

25. **February 22**

Most don't know the dominance level of their souls, so taking the February 19 truth into consideration is valuable.

26. **February 23**

The body can become sick from ordinary thoughts that are self-blaming in nature.

27. **February 24**

When the body becomes sick, it is a reminder from your true self, your soul, to take it easy.

28. **February 25**

Taking it easy on your body is in alignment with I Am.

29. February 26

I Am loves being you.

30. February 27

I Am loves all of the things you love.

31. February 28

I Am understands things the character doesn't love.

32. February 29 (Leap Year)

The body is a symbol of unity between the divine and the mortal.

March: Gratitude

1. The soul expresses gratitude on a constant basis. It is primarily concerned with service, so its gratitude tends to center around service opportunities. It remains grateful for a mere sliver of hope that its mind-body vehicle will heed its advice. It is joyful beyond description when it does. Who does the soul show gratitude towards? Life itself, the largest soul collective, and itself. It is thankful for its opportunities to grow and develop, however challenging those opportunities may be. It is grateful to itself for its willingness to take on life's challenges and deal with sometimes exceedingly difficult characters who oppose the soul's viewpoint at every turn.

2. On the surface level, the character level, there is much to be thankful for. And all thankfulness emanates from the soul level. Souls are

grateful for all acts of kindness, both small and large, especially the ones where there is nothing in it for anyone's gain. It is just done as a kind and helpful act, with no reward or anything expected in return. You can see these everywhere you look. From both individuals and organized groups doing things for others, to entire countries giving humanitarian aid to countries in need. Souls shine during these moments, until the darkness settles in again and the character switches back to the "me, myself, and I" mode once again. Moments of gratitude give souls hope that one day they will have a starring role and can usurp the ego once and for all.

3. **Guidelines**: Readers should delve directly into the "Gift of Wisdom" after completing all of the "Steps to Authenticity." Simply find the appropriate starting date on the calendar and begin there. Each month of affirmations centers around the theme and each theme is an aspect of wisdom. At the conclusion of this second year, the gift of wisdom will be yours. These exercises will facilitate soul growth by quieting the mind and retraining it to be in service to the soul and not strictly to the ego. Godspeed to all those who tread these waters to refine their authentic selves into shimmering gems.

4. ## March 1

I Am grateful for you until you realize that we are one.

5. ## March 2

I Am you.

6. ## March 3

Every step you take in the name of love brings you closer to me.

7. March 4

I Am grateful for all of the challenging times you have provided for me.

8. March 5

I Am grateful for all of the tender moments we have shared.

9. March 6

I Am grateful for the good times and the bad times.

10. March 7

The hard times may have been your greatest teacher.

11. March 8

The hard times point you to me.

12. March 9

The good times are breaks from life's hard lessons.

13. March 10

Life knows what we need to experience before we can merge as one.

14. March 11

Merging as one cohesive, individual expression of God is the goal.

15. March 12

Merging as one cohesive, individual expression of God is everyone's goal, whether they realize it or not.

16. ## March 13

I was the one who comforted you on the worst day of your life.

17. ## March 14

I was the one who tapped you on the shoulder and reminded you to not do what your ego was telling you to do.

18. ## March 15

I was there when you had your first kiss.

19. ## March 16

I was there when you had to explain your bad behavior to your parents.

20. ## March 17

I always help you to look on the bright side.

21. ## March 18

All optimism originates from me.

22. ## March 19

When you are grateful, it is because I brought something to your attention and you listened.

23. ## March 20

When others in your life experience are grateful for you, it's because they see me in you.

24. ## March 21

When others see me in you, they will start to see their own souls.

25. ## March 22

The soul is what the entire earth project is all about.

26. ## March 23

The soul is the only thing that truly matters in the end.

27. ## March 24

The soul is the only thing that truly matters in the end because the soul is part of God.

28. ## March 25

God and its helpmate, the resistance to God, are the only things here.

29. ## March 26

Of the two things described in the March 25 affirmation, only one of them is real.

30. ## March 27

Only God is real.

31. ## March 28

God is real because it is eternal.

32. ## March 29

God is real because it is the light that will never go out.

33. ## March 30

The resistance to God is a temporary mechanism for soul growth and is a temporary illusion.

34. **March 31**

Complete gratitude arrives when you eventually realize that we are one and the same. The character will fade away but the true you will live forever.

April: Awareness

1. Awareness is knowledge of all things, seen and unseen. It is the ability to sense the underbelly, to smell content that your senses are not alerting you to. Awareness is commonly known as the sixth sense. When yours has developed enough that you have become aware of it, you can thank your soul. Awareness from a mature soul is awareness from God. It will notify, alert, suggest, remind, and guide you towards or away from events, characters, or situations that may be helpful, or should be avoided at all costs. The resistance to God or love is very strong here and is potentially dangerous. Awareness always leads to the sixth sense of knowing and being able to discern between what is love and what isn't. Oftentimes the five senses fail to do this.

2. The resistance to love is volatile. Awareness helps characters to navigate the often-choppy waters of living on the planet earth as a human. If love is not flowing in an individual or community the results are combustible. Steering clear of these situations helps souls to focus the character on opening up to love, without buying into the fear narrative in the collective. Souls do not need to be protected from anything, but characters do need to be protected from outside influences. The body itself is a huge investment for a soul. Awareness is a gift that guarantees

that the investment will remain as a container for soul growth and not get shut down by the world's negativity.

3. **Guidelines**: Readers should delve directly into the "Gift of Wisdom" after completing all of the "Steps to Authenticity." Simply find the appropriate starting date on the calendar and begin there. Each month of affirmations centers around the theme and each theme is an aspect of wisdom. At the conclusion of this second year, the gift of wisdom will be yours. These exercises will facilitate soul growth by quieting the mind and retraining it to be in service to the soul and not strictly to the ego. Godspeed to all those who tread these waters to refine their authentic selves into shimmering gems.

4. April 1

I point you in the correct direction through awareness.

5. April 2

Do you remember that time when you almost did something cataclysmic but didn't? You have me to thank for that.

6. April 3

Do you remember that time when you were involved in a heated conversation and walked away? You were listening to me by disengaging.

7. April 4

I Am your best guide during a time of crisis.

8. April 5

I Am your best friend, only concerned with your well-being and safety.

9. April 6

I prompt you to choose the opportunity where I can express love to the greatest possible degree.

10. April 7

I help you to see situations as they are, not as you hope they will be.

11. April 8

I help you to see the true content of your past.

12. April 9

I help you to see the true content of the world's past.

13. April 10

Awareness and vision are one and the same.

14. April 11

Vision is seeing clearly.

15. April 12

I know things that you don't know as a character.

16. April 13

Besides keeping you safe, awareness cues you in to the story behind the story.

17. April 14

Awareness guides you to say just the right thing at the right time.

18. **April 15**

Awareness guides you to do just the right thing at the right time.

19. **April 16**

Wisdom is incomplete without awareness.

20. **April 17**

Awareness isn't too cautious or too enthusiastic. It approaches all things with a firm sense of knowing.

21. **April 18**

Awareness is compassionate.

22. **April 19**

Awareness connects observations about situations and individuals with an "I've been there" type of commonality.

23. **April 20**

I Am saying "I want to show something to you" through awareness.

24. **April 21**

I Am saying "I want to say something to you" through awareness.

25. **April 22**

I primarily communicate to you through feelings.

26. **April 23**

When I communicate to you through thoughts, you will know that this is the final frontier.

27. April 24

When I Am in the final frontier, I Am in control of you and start to merge with you, becoming one and the same.

28. April 25

Awareness is a step towards my independence from your tyranny.

29. April 26

Awareness lets you know that you aren't who you think you are but are something else entirely.

30. April 27

God looks out of your eyes.

31. April 28

The blind are those who don't know what God is.

32. April 29

The blind are those who don't know where God is.

33. April 30

I Am you.

May: Serenity

1. Wisdom is a package deal, as the soul takes reign of the body. It has twelve different elements, and serenity is the one featured for May's exercises. The inner peace that was referred to in the original *A Course in Miracles* will now be known as serenity. Serenity is only one of the twelve strands of wisdom. It isn't something to achieve as a goal. It is a gift in and of itself and is a part of a much larger gift. What is serenity? It is the calm in the storm. It is the quietness inside a rainy afternoon. It is knowing that, despite appearances, all is well. All is as it must be.

2. **Guidelines**: Readers should delve directly into the "Gift of Wisdom" after completing all of the "Steps to Authenticity." Simply find the appropriate starting date on the calendar and begin there. Each month of affirmations centers around the theme and each theme is an aspect of wisdom. At the conclusion of this second year, the gift of wisdom will be yours. These exercises will facilitate soul growth by quieting the mind and retraining it to be in service to the soul and not strictly to the ego. Godspeed to all those who tread these waters to refine their authentic selves into shimmering gems.

3. May 1

Peace is always an option.

4. May 2

Serenity is sometimes a leap of faith.

5. May 3

Peace does not come from denying that something is real. It comes from knowing that more of God will grow from the combustion.

6. May 4

I will guide you on what to say or do.

7. May 5

Find your place of serenity and listen to me.

8. May 6

I live inside a serene state of mind, not one caught up emotionally over appearances.

9. May 7

Return to an especially tumultuous period in your most recent lifetime. Were you able to find me in stillness?

10. May 8

If another tumultuous period were to revisit you, would you be able to find me?

11. May 9

I Am here at all times, in all places.

12. May 10

I Am beneath thought.

13. May 11

Thought has the temporary ability to block my power.

14. May 12

Thought has the temporary ability to block the power of God.

15. May 13

Serenity helps you process the hard aspects of life.

16. May 14

Serenity isn't a goal; it is a tool.

17. May 15

The power of the soul can't be accessed without serenity.

18. May 16

A chaotic mind cannot access the soul.

19. May 17

A chaotic mind cannot access God.

20. May 18

Praying to God produces mixed results because the mind is not clear.

21. May 19

A mind that is not clear cannot know itself.

22. May 20

The mind is designed to be utilized in service to the soul.

23. May 21

The soul cannot tell the mind what to say or do if chaos reigns.

24. May 22

If the mind thinks it is separate from the soul, it will take time to heal this fundamental misunderstanding.

25. May 23

All healing comes from switching your identity from ego to soul.

26. May 24

The process of merging your identity with your soul is commonly known as awakening.

27. May 25

Can you see the importance of serenity?

28. May 26

Serenity is a quiet mind.

29. May 27

God can talk to a quiet mind.

30. May 28

A loud mind cannot hear its own soul.

31. May 29

Your soul is always trying to talk to you. I will never stop trying.

32. May 30

There is nothing you could ever do or say to keep me from you because I Am you.

33. May 31

Serenity is a pathway to God.

June: Peace

1. The soul is serene and offers this gift to the character, as an offering prior to consumption when it becomes a way of life. The same can be said of all twelve strands of wisdom, but none as important as the one for the month of June, which is peace. Peace is the opposite of conflict, and war is an extreme form of conflict. War is always a possibility with ego-led characters. Conflict can get violent rapidly among individuals or groups and can become violent slowly over time with entire nations of individuals. The gift of peace is the manifestation of serenity, which is an internal quality of the soul. Peace is an external quality when the soul has consumed the form it is operating. The body becomes incapable of acting on the ego's violent and aggressive tendencies.

2. Soul-driven characters are peaceful and not involved in conflict. The same cannot be said about ego-driven characters who are soul emergent. Walking away from an argument or fight means that steps were taken towards an argument or a fight. But souls only love, so they would not have engaged in the precursors. Souls don't feel like there is anything to defend, because love does not need to be defended. Everything else stems from the ego and the illusionary identity of being solely human, where property ownership and philosophical beliefs need protection. Having internal serenity and external peace are both gifts that lead to longevity as a human. Both are priceless.

3. **Guidelines**: Readers should delve directly into the "Gift of Wisdom" after completing all of the "Steps to Authenticity." Simply find the appropriate starting date on the calendar and begin there. Each month of affirmations centers around the theme and each theme is an aspect of wisdom. At the conclusion of this second year, the gift of wisdom will be yours. These exercises will facilitate soul growth by quieting the mind and retraining it to be in service to the soul and not strictly to the ego. Godspeed to all those who tread these waters to refine their authentic selves into shimmering gems.

4. June 1

There is nothing here worth fighting over.

5. June 2

The only thing of real value cannot be taken from you.

6. June 3

Nothing can happen to your soul.

7. June 4

Your soul will protect its canister (your body) if it needs protection.

8. June 5

Listening to your soul will keep you safe.

9. June 6

The soul promotes peace during even the most difficult of circumstances.

10. June 7

The adage to Do No Harm is an instruction from the soul collective to promote peace.

11. June 8

Engaging in warfare through words or actions is counterproductive to peace.

12. June 9

The ego believes wholeheartedly that warfare is sometimes necessary to protect what is rightfully yours.

13. June 10

The ego believes wholeheartedly that warfare is sometimes necessary to keep others at bay.

14. June 11

The soul only believes in peace.

15. June 12

I was the voice of reason during times of madness in your current lifetime.

16. June 13

Some characters regret listening to their souls because they didn't get a feeling of satisfaction from following their instinct to strike back.

17. June 14

Telling children to hit back reinforces their natural urges to do so.

18. **June 15**

Walk away and forgive are always messages the soul promotes.

19. **June 16**

Ego-dominant individuals view soul-dominant individuals as weak.

20. **June 17**

Defenselessness refers to disarming the ego and body. I will protect you if danger is nearby.

21. **June 18**

Listen to me and I will guide you in all things.

22. **June 19**

You can feel peaceful even when bills are due and there are no funds to pay them.

23. **June 20**

You can feel peaceful even when there is no food in the pantry.

24. **June 21**

You can feel peaceful no matter what is happening.

25. **June 22**

Peace is my gift to you.

26. **June 23**

You can choose to open my gifts to you and discover their usefulness.

27. June 24

One day you will discover that you are peace.

28. June 25

You are me.

29. June 26

I do not promote or condone any type of arguing or bickering.

30. June 27

I do not promote or condone any type of physical fighting.

31. June 28

Peace is my middle name.

32. June 29

Love and peace both seem like such radical concepts to the ego.

33. June 30

I cannot do anything to harm a vessel that contains another part of myself (God).

July: Enjoyment

1. Life, on the surface, can be fun for both soul-emergent and soul-dominant characters. It can be filled with excitement, intrigue, mystery,

and suspense. Characters can work hard to achieve any goals they may have and then enjoy the fruits of said labors. There are many paths here and many choices. Even finding the right path may take some doing. The soul is part of every life experience, and it always encourages its mind-body vehicle to stop and smell the roses along the way. The ego gets caught up in the details, the minutiae, and makes the journey harder and more unpleasant than it needs to be. Enjoyment of life's journeys is of paramount importance, especially now that you know the secret of life. Life and all its myriad journeys are designed for the merging with, and eventual consumption of, the ego. Only then can life really begin.

2. **Guidelines**: Readers should delve directly into the "Gift of Wisdom" after completing all of the "Steps to Authenticity." Simply find the appropriate starting date on the calendar and begin there. Each month of affirmations centers around the theme and each theme is an aspect of wisdom. At the conclusion of this second year, the gift of wisdom will be yours. These exercises will facilitate soul growth by quieting the mind and retraining it to be in service to the soul and not strictly to the ego. Godspeed to all those who tread these waters to refine their authentic selves into shimmering gems.

3. July 1

   If I want you to be happy (and I do) then God wants you to be happy because we are one and the same.

4. July 2

   Living a life of love brings joy.

5. July 3

   The only thing that wants you to be miserable is the ego.

6. ## July 4

The ego doesn't know how to make you happy.

7. ## July 5

The ego tries this and then that in an effort to make you happy.

8. ## July 6

Everything the ego does is temporary.

9. ## July 7

The soul's love doesn't need bells and whistles. It is complete in and of itself.

10. ## July 8

The joy that comes from love is unmatched by anything the ego has to offer.

11. ## July 9

I want you to be happy all the time.

12. ## July 10

Every day is special to me.

13. ## July 11

Every day is special to all souls.

14. ## July 12

Joy is worry free.

15. July 13

There are ways to find joy, even in times of sorrow.

16. July 14

The enjoyment of life costs nothing.

17. July 15

The ego wants you to believe that life is a struggle.

18. July 16

I want you to know that life is about finding joy.

19. July 17

Enjoy now and leave the past in the past.

20. July 18

Enjoy now and leave the future in the future.

21. July 19

The ego has shown you joy, but it doesn't last.

22. July 20

The ego's version of joy is dependent on external things being a certain way.

23. July 21

The joy I want to share with you is not dependent on anything being a certain way.

24. July 22

My joy is not a slave to time.

25. July 23

There can be joy in misery and sadness if you are present and open.

26. July 24

Joy comes from knowing what is real.

27. July 25

When you look at the hard things in life through the eyes of the ego, you will not find joy.

28. July 26

When you look at the hard things in life through my vision, you will find reasons to be joyful.

29. July 27

Joy costs nothing but is invaluable.

30. July 28

Joy comes from seeing purpose in your life.

31. July 29

Joy comes from seeing purpose in the lives of others.

32. July 30

Joy comes from seeing purpose in all of life's myriad forms.

33. **July 31**

When you allow yourself to merge with me, joy will follow

August: Solitude

1. If you are not wholly human but are a soul, an aspect of the divine source of everything, how could you ever need anyone to complete you? In solitude, you have absolutely everything. You feel whole and connected while being alone or by being in fellowship with others. You have the choice, but being with others isn't an obligation or requirement. It is the human animal that feels compelled to have social interaction and to enter into different types of relationships out of need. I'll scratch your back if you scratch mine is the way of the world with soul-emergent characters, but soul-dominant characters don't feel compelled to engage in this type of a codependent relationship. Being comfortable in solitude is one of the twelve strands of wisdom and is a gift to the character to free them from conditional relationships of all types. The soul is complete and doesn't need anything from characters. Its needs will be met because God never fails to fulfill its own needs.

2. **Guidelines**: Readers should delve directly into the "Gift of Wisdom" after completing all of the "Steps to Authenticity." Simply find the appropriate starting date on the calendar and begin there. Each month of affirmations centers around the theme and each theme is an aspect of wisdom. At the conclusion of this second year, the gift of wisdom will be yours. These exercises will facilitate soul growth by quieting the mind and retraining it to be in service to the soul and not strictly to the ego.

Godspeed to all those who tread these waters to refine their authentic selves into shimmering gems.

3. **August 1**

I only want you to be happy.

4. **August 2**

The gift of solitude will help you realize where true happiness originates from.

5. **August 3**

The gift of solitude will bring you closer to me.

6. **August 4**

Being closer to me will promote merging as one.

7. **August 5**

After we merge as one, the ego will be consumed.

8. **August 6**

Being by yourself doesn't have to be lonely.

9. **August 7**

In solitude, you need nothing.

10. **August 8**

There is joy in solitude.

11. **August 9**

Spending quality time with others is icing on the cake, not the cake itself.

12. **August 10**

The relationship you have with me is the most valuable one you can have.

13. **August 11**

When you merge with me and identify as soul, you will be a free spirit.

14. **August 12**

When you merge with me and identify as soul, you will discover that there is no loss in love. You will bring your human gifts and foibles with you.

15. **August 13**

I was with you when no one else was.

16. **August 14**

Together, we make good decisions.

17. **August 15**

Separately from me, you make bad decisions.

18. **August 16**

I'm the one you want in your corner. I will tell you to give up the fight and walk away with me as your guide.

19. August 17

You and I have no one to fight.

20. August 18

You and I have nothing to fight.

21. August 19

It's better to be alone in solitude than to be surrounded by chaos and insanity.

22. August 20

Love flows in solitude.

23. August 21

Fear thrives in chaos and insanity.

24. August 22

I'm your best friend.

25. August 23

I always have your best interests in consideration.

26. August 24

Other characters can be your friends, but a soul mate or soul mates offer a much deeper connection.

27. August 25

Soul mates can enjoy being in a state of solitude with one another.

28. August 26

Soul mates are always soul dominant.

29. August 27

Soul mates are always old souls or mature souls.

30. August 28

Solitude promotes the stillness that is necessary to hear and know my wisdom.

31. August 29

Together we can move mountains.

32. August 30

In a state of separation from me, you can move food from one side of the plate to the other.

33. August 31

Merging with me is the wise choice.

September: Togetherness

1. Togetherness is the opposite of separation. Togetherness is unity and unity always starts with the body being unified with, and not in opposition to, the soul. From there, togetherness or unity involves unification with everything and everyone – those who are in a state

of unity with their own souls, the vast majority who are not, and untethered souls who create freely without bodies. Togetherness is a gift of wisdom, a strand of wisdom that promotes the "we're all in this together" type of attitude, rather than the ego's attitude of us vs. them and me vs. you. It is cooperative and not competitive. It sees the glass as half full and not half empty. It sees everyone as a work in progress and not the sum of their shortcomings and mistakes. Togetherness promotes seeing yourself in everyone, the good and the bad, the holy and the evil. Togetherness is a lot of things and honesty is at the top of the list.

2. **Guidelines**: Readers should delve directly into the "Gift of Wisdom" after completing all of the "Steps to Authenticity." Simply find the appropriate starting date on the calendar and begin there. Each month of affirmations centers around the theme and each theme is an aspect of wisdom. At the conclusion of this second year, the gift of wisdom will be yours. These exercises will facilitate soul growth by quieting the mind and retraining it to be in service to the soul and not strictly to the ego. Godspeed to all those who tread these waters to refine their authentic selves into shimmering gems.

3. September 1

Togetherness includes separateness.

4. September 2

Separateness is the crux of the problem here.

5. September 3

Separateness dictates that someone is somewhere you are not.

6. September 4

Togetherness acknowledges that someone is somewhere you are not, but there is another acknowledgement of sameness.

7. September 5

Even those who speak different languages have commonality in togetherness and not being the other.

8. September 6

Togetherness is the way love sees the world and all of its people and cultures.

9. September 7

Separateness puts everything in distinct categories.

10. September 8

Separateness puts everyone in distinct categories.

11. September 9

Togetherness eschews strict categorization.

12. September 10

Togetherness eschews all arbitrary boundaries.

13. September 11

Seeing the humanness and soulness of the stranger is what togetherness promotes.

14. September 12

Being a stranger is never a permanent problem when togetherness is in charge.

15. September 13

I will help you to be together in unity with everyone.

16. September 14

You can feel togetherness with anyone.

17. September 15

You can feel togetherness with everyone.

18. September 16

Togetherness always leads to unity.

19. September 17

Togetherness is a precursor to unity.

20. September 18

Separation builds walls and togetherness disintegrates them.

21. September 19

There isn't anything someone could tell you that you won't understand on some level, thanks to togetherness.

22. September 20

There isn't anything someone could do that you won't understand on some level, thanks to togetherness.

23. September 21

Judgment and condemnation prevent togetherness.

24. September 22

Judgment and condemnation block my free expression.

25. September 23

Judgment and condemnation are part of the ego's belief in separation.

26. September 24

Nonjudgment and acceptance of all is a crucial aspect of togetherness.

27. September 25

I teach you togetherness through my acceptance of you.

28. September 26

I teach you togetherness through my nonjudgment of you.

29. September 27

First comes togetherness and then comes unity.

30. September 28

There is nothing you can't accept and understand through togetherness.

31. September 29

Nothing is off limits, out of bounds, through togetherness.

32. September 30

When you practice the gift of togetherness towards others, it will help you merge with me.

October: Wholeness

1. Wholeness simply means whole or holy. It is the unification of God with man. Wholeness is integration of divine intelligence with immortality, with human thinking, with human emotions, and with mortality into one cohesive unit where the soul reigns supreme. It is not one or the other. It is all of the above. All of the boxes are checked and love, not fear, fuels everything. This is the goal of this course, for you to return to wholeness – the state you left when you incarnated here. But this time you are enveloping your human self and in doing so are healing the rift. To be whole or holy means that healing is complete. The need for it isn't there anymore. There are no more symptoms or effects from the absence of the soul's influence. You are one complete entity that is one very small part of one complete entity. In wholeness, God has made one more significant step in the earth's project, where love is all there will be in the end. Love will have finally conquered fear. Wholeness and unity will be all that remain. End of game. Game over.

2. **Guidelines**: Readers should delve directly into the "Gift of Wisdom" after completing all of the "Steps to Authenticity." Simply find the appropriate starting date on the calendar and begin there. Each month of affirmations centers around the theme and each theme is an aspect

of wisdom. At the conclusion of this second year, the gift of wisdom will be yours. These exercises will facilitate soul growth by quieting the mind and retraining it to be in service to the soul and not strictly to the ego. Godspeed to all those who tread these waters to refine their authentic selves into shimmering gems.

3. October 1

I Am not now, nor have I ever been, broken.

4. October 2

The human self is a wounded self.

5. October 3

The human self is a broken piece of fine china, taped together with packing tape.

6. October 4

Life activating a human body has never harmed me in any way, shape, or form.

7. October 5

When you were laying in a hospital bed, I was fine.

8. October 6

We have been two different things for much of your lifetime.

9. October 7

The awareness of the presence of the soul varies greatly from person to person.

10. **October 8**

In some characters, the soul has been the uninvited guest.

11. **October 9**

In some characters, the soul has been the one you have to invite, out of a sense of obligation.

12. **October 10**

In a few characters, the soul is a treasured friend.

13. **October 11**

I want to be more than a treasured friend to you.

14. **October 12**

My goal is for you to finally realize that I Am you.

15. **October 13**

The purpose of your character is to lead you to me or better put, lead you to you, the real you.

16. **October 14**

When we have merged, I will still have your name, as well as your personal and family history.

17. **October 15**

When we have merged, I will still like all of the things you like.

18. **October 16**

When we have merged, I will still not like all of the things you don't like, but that won't stop me from trying to change your mind.

19. October 17

When we have merged, in wholeness and unity, I will advocate for you to explore all of the things in life you haven't wanted to explore before.

20. October 18

Once we have become a unified force, life will be our playground in which to explore love.

21. October 19

Love will give you a new lease on life.

22. October 20

Love always says yes to love.

23. October 21

Not everything in the human world reflects love, but many things do.

24. October 22

Together, we can shine light on everything and see what's really there.

25. October 23

Love will show you what is valuable.

26. October 24

Love will show you what is invaluable.

27. October 25

Love will show you what can be discarded.

28. October 26

Love is the standard bearer.

29. October 27

Everything is either love or not love yet.

30. October 28

Everyone is either love or not love yet.

31. October 29

There is much I want to show you.

32. October 30

Your ego has prevented you from hearing my voice.

33. October 31

The day you seriously start to listen to me is the day your life will start over again because the reset button will have been pushed.

November: Kindness

1. Love is the same as God and I Am the same as God. The only difference is that I Am not the totality of God, as I Am only an infinitesimally small

part of God. God is a highly sophisticated and complex network or web. Whether you are referring to the complex network or just a soul aspect, God is always kind, as love is always kind. Love is not heavy handed. We are talking about the only true type of love there is, unconditional love. And it may surprise you to discover how strong this type of love is. It is intolerant of nonsense and very comfortable with tough love. However, the concern for others is always reflected with kindness in everything God does. God is only interested in growing more of itself, and therefore, it is supportive and kind. If God wore a shirt, it would be given off its figurative back, since God doesn't have a back, but you get the point. Even when God takes corrective action of any type, it is done with kindness, not from a place of weakness.

2. **Guidelines**: Readers should delve directly into the "Gift of Wisdom" after completing all of the "Steps to Authenticity." Simply find the appropriate starting date on the calendar and begin there. Each month of affirmations centers around the theme and each theme is an aspect of wisdom. At the conclusion of this second year, the gift of wisdom will be yours. These exercises will facilitate soul growth by quieting the mind and retraining it to be in service to the soul and not strictly to the ego. Godspeed to all those who tread these waters to refine their authentic selves into shimmering gems.

3. November 1

The ego is anything but kind.

4. November 2

If the ego is kind, it wants something in return.

5. November 3

I Am always kind.

6. November 4

I Am always kind because I love you.

7. November 5

Kindness is exceedingly patient.

8. November 6

Being unkind is just another sign of not understanding.

9. November 7

Love is kind, even if it has a strongly worded message.

10. November 8

Ego-dominant characters respond better to kindness than to harsh rhetoric.

11. November 9

Kindness helps smooth things over.

12. November 10

There is never justification for being unkind.

13. November 11

No one is ever deserving of unkind treatment.

14. November 12

When you remember to treat others as you expect to be treated, you will remember how important kindness is.

15. November 13

You are more likely to remember those who showed you kindness when you didn't think you deserved it.

16. November 14

It is the small acts of kindness that help bring a smile to someone's face.

17. November 15

The more soul dominant you are, the kinder you will be.

18. November 16

Kindness and gentleness are the best of friends.

19. November 17

Unkindness only makes things worse.

20. November 18

I only want you to be kind to yourself.

21. November 19

I only want you to be kind to others.

22. November 20

When you are kind during the hard times, you will teach others an invaluable lesson.

23. November 21

When you are kind during the easy, breezy times, you will teach others how they can be in the world.

24. November 22

Kindness is contagious.

25. November 23

Unkindness and love are not compatible.

26. November 24

When a character is unkind, its soul is calling for love in the form of outside reinforcements.

27. November 25

Children who are treated with kindness will grow up to be adults who treat others with kindness.

28. November 26

Children who are treated with kindness will grow up to be soul-dominant individuals.

29. November 27

A kind gesture here and there never harmed anyone.

30. November 28

Only kindness is the same as only love.

31. November 29

Kindness is quick to forget unkindness.

32. November 30

Unkindness only produces more unkindness.

December: Wisdom

1. Wisdom is both a strand and a totality. As a strand, it is a right course of action. As a totality, it is the sum of all its parts: Patience, Consideration for the Body, Gratitude, Awareness, Serenity, Peace, Enjoyment, Solitude, Togetherness, Wholeness, Kindness, and right course of action. The definition of wisdom in its totality is the embodiment of the soul, the marriage of the body with the soul. Both its advice and way of being are sage. It understands fear but does not engage with it. It sees all individual and collective problems as separation from the soul. A wise "old soul" if you will, models the merging of the ego with the soul, and the ego's eventual consumption, with love as its guide. The following exercises for December concern both the strand definition of wisdom and the totality definition.

2. **Guidelines**: Readers should delve directly into the "Gift of Wisdom" after completing all of the "Steps to Authenticity." Simply find the appropriate starting date on the calendar and begin there. Each month of affirmations centers around the theme and each theme is an aspect of wisdom. At the conclusion of this second year, the gift of wisdom will be yours. These exercises will facilitate soul growth by quieting the mind and retraining it to be in service to the soul and not strictly to the ego. Godspeed to all those who tread these waters to refine their authentic selves into shimmering gems.

3. December 1

Doing the right thing at the right time is because of wisdom.

4. December 2

Foolishness is the opposite of wisdom.

5. December 3

People who do foolish things are not listening to their souls.

6. December 4

When you follow my advice, there will be the best possible outcomes for all involved.

7. December 5

The foolish path is filled with lessons that involve suffering.

8. December 6

Suffering can lead to wisdom, after graduating from the school of hard knocks.

9. December 7

A wise, soul-dominant individual has overcome their foolish tendencies.

10. December 8

Wise, soul-dominant individuals were once fools but had the sense to start listening to what life was telling them.

11. December 9

A wise one would never judge and condemn anyone for being a fool. Wise ones are honest in all things.

12. December 10

If a wise one isn't sure what to do in any situation, they know that the wise course of action is to wait until they have the clarity to move forward.

13. December 11

Now that two years have passed, how have you changed?

14. December 12

Now that two years have passed, what value does living a soul-dominant life have for you?

15. December 13

Do you see the value in listening to me?

16. December 14

Have there been any harmful attitudes you have let go of since starting to listen to me?

17. December 15

How do you see me? As an enhancement, or as a goody two shoes?

18. December 16

I Am the divine aspect of you until you become the divine aspect.

19. December 17

The divine is the deeper part of you.

20. December 18

Good and bad are too simplistic when referring to the soul and the ego.

21. December 19

Twelve different qualities or strands have opened up in you now.

22. December 20

Life will be different with me at the helm.

23. December 21

Life will be different with love as your focus.

24. December 22

Wisdom is my gift to you.

25. December 23

Wisdom and love are the same.

26. December 24

Wisdom will never stop revealing life's secrets to you.

27. December 25

Wisdom will bring good things into your life.

28. December 26

Having the gift of wisdom is an example of the As Within, So Without spiritual concept.

29. December 27

If you have had a wise one in your life experience, you have most certainly been positively affected by their presence.

30. December 28

Now that you are a wise soul, you will enhance any situation.

31. December 29

Now that you are a wise soul, you will enhance or bless any relationship.

32. December 30

Wise ones create by extending love everywhere they go.

33. December 31

You are a Creator now.

Epilogue

1. For the first year, in Chapter Seven, "Steps to Authenticity," I explained twelve basic concepts to you: the character who is using the body's brain to process the information I presented. In the daily exercises, you were able to reflect on things that may have been long buried, important things that needed to be released. In the second year, it is your own soul who is speaking to you, wanting to get your attention and develop a closer relationship with you. All souls here want to say the same things,

so the exercises are generic and yet they apply to absolutely everyone. There is no one to whom these exercises do not apply. These exercises can be uncomfortable, but there is freedom in discomfort. You will never be free enough to embrace your own true identity unless you take a good look at your own ego or false sense of self.

Chapter Nine

The Doors and Pathways to Understanding

Introduction

1. This chapter of *Soul in the Driver's Seat: A Course in Miracles for Today, Volume One* is a collection of short essays on various topics from the viewpoint of the soul.

Prayer

2. What is prayer? Is it begging and pleading with God to help with whatever situation you find yourself in? Is it the bowed-head confessional, asking for forgiveness? Is it the ritual of communion or sacred rights? Do you have to use an intermediary to communicate with God? Does God pay attention more if you get on your hands and knees, while tears and screams pierce the air? These are legitimate questions as they are all common practices, but they are all based on false beliefs. You don't have to look far for God because it is inside you in the form of a soul, and everyone has full and completely free access. Your soul is all knowing. It knows everything about you. It knows more about you than you do. You don't have to go to a church or a confessional booth because God isn't there unless you are. God goes where you go. If you want to speak to the Divine, quiet your mind and speak. It hears every word whether silent or said aloud. It will answer you with love and clarity and a simple request to keep talking in unity and

relationship. God has waited for this day for a long time. God wants to walk forward with you as a full partner, until the day comes when you are ready to blend and become God, walking the earth as the Divine and the mortal. What is prayer? There is only one. It asks the soul, "What should I do next?"

Sin

3. What is sin? Is it a transgression against God? Who can transgress against God? The resistance to God comes from the ego, which is designed to resist the soul. Characters can choose their own egos over their own souls. Does this mean they have sinned against God? Since God is the soul and the totality of all souls, does it judge and condemn characters it sees as being in opposition to it? Do souls judge and condemn their mind-body vehicles? Characters are free to choose ego over soul, but does that imply that they have sinned? In fact, it only means that they have acted naturally, according to their natural programming. So, no, characters cannot sin or commit any act that God sees as requiring forgiveness. You know enough about God by now to know that it is only loving and supportive of its host characters. It is never judgmental. Characters are quite capable of committing unloving acts that are not in accordance with love, with their own souls, with God. This just means, however, that they still have a long way to go before their souls can emerge from the darkness of the ego and come to the forefront. Characters make mistakes when they choose ego over soul or fear over love, but all mistakes are learning opportunities. God does not forgive because it doesn't condemn in the first place. Therefore, sin is a man-made concept, not a spiritual truth.

Healing

4. There is a point in the transformation from being entirely ego-led to

being entirely soul-led, when there is simply nothing left to be healed. There are no more effects stemming from the ego's separation from the soul and arrogant attitude about it. There is no more disease. There is no more pain or depression or anger. There is nothing that wants to be numbed by drugs or alcohol. There is no regret. There is no living in the past. There are no lingering questions about why this happened or that happened. There is only acceptance. There is only peace. There is only joy. If there is a reward at the end of the transformation, at the point that you the butterfly is ready to fly, it is this. You are healed and you are free. You are ready to experience life in a brand-new way, as love incarnate.

Sanity vs. Insanity

5. In the original *A Course in Miracles*, all ego-led characters were described as being insane. This was inaccurate, especially since mental illness is such a big concern in your society. There are healthy, functional egos in the world, who listen to their souls on Easter and Christmas. And there are dysfunctional egos with a host of problematic behavioral and thought-related problems who are self-destructive in nature. They can even become destructive towards others. This is the truth of the human world. One could argue that the ratio of functional to dysfunctional has changed over time, and that the dysfunctional group has grown to astronomical proportions. My point is that all fear-based thoughts and behavior is insane when it is compared with love-based thoughts and behavior which is sane. The degree to which a character is listening to their soul is the true measure of sanity.

Presence vs. Image

6. Image is everywhere in the material world. It is used to sell products. It is used by the ego to sell itself to others but mostly to itself. The ego

believes tooth and nail that it is a body, so body image is of paramount importance to the ego. The soul, on the other hand, always feels good. This feeling or state of being is what is known as presence. Presence doesn't want anything from anyone. It doesn't care if someone doesn't like the way they style their hair or if they wear the most fashionable clothes or even if they wear clean clothes or no clothes. Presence feels good, and this is the element that is projected. Presence doesn't try to do anything. It just is. It does not care one iota about what anyone thinks. It just says "hello" without a care in the world. Image is composed of attached thoughts. Presence is unattached Being. It just is.

Acceptance vs. Resistance

7. The soul accepts things the character can't or won't accept. It accepts the unacceptable. The ego gets on its high horse and raises a clenched fist at the unfairness and unacceptableness of any situation, but the soul just looks for the silver lining. Egos can get upset over tiny upsets in life. The spilled milk on the new dress can make a character's blood boil. But it really isn't the spilled milk that is causing the anger. It's the cumulative effect of a lifetime of spilled-milk incidents. Characters are never angry about that which they express anger about. Repressed anger can be even more dangerous to the body and to the character's frame of mind. The soul just smiles about whatever life is serving up. It resists nothing because it knows that its control is only in its response. The soul only chooses how to love difficult situations or difficult people. The ego only reacts and resists. Acceptance and resistance are two different ways of being from two different ways of being.

Innocence vs. Guilt

8. Souls are one hundred percent innocent, one hundred percent of the time. They never promote anything that would produce guilt in the

character. As you know from your experience, guilt is a built-in mechanism. It is a wayshower. It tells you what not to do. Once it has done its job it needs to be released. Guilt is part of a healthy ego. Unhealthy egos do not have significant amounts of guilt and are said to be unconscionable or psychotic. The term *you are innocent* from *A Course in Miracles* refers to you, the soul. Egos are anything but innocent. They accidentally and intentionally inflict harm on themselves and on others. They can be self-destructive or destructive, period. Know the difference. In this world, you are an ego and are susceptible to guilt, until you have transformed to soul. Guilt is released through understanding and forgiveness.

Response vs. Reaction

9. Love responds and fear reacts. Fear wants to endlessly talk about what happened and who is to blame. Love is just concerned about what needs are there and possible ways to help. These are very different approaches, as are all dilemmas between the ego and the soul. Fear wants to prevent difficult things from happening again. Love knows it doesn't have that kind of power, and that it would be a waste of energy to focus on possible negative future outcomes. Love is always present in the now aspect of time, which is the only time there is. Love only responds now. Fear is seldom present now and focuses mostly on the past or on the future. Reaction is about self-protection. Reaction is about being offended. Response is concerned with extending love to love. Response is how the soul supports other souls, strengthening them in the process.

Relationships Empowered

10. Nothing will empower a relationship like love will – pure unconditional love between souls. Like won't do it, and human love has an expiration date on it. Unconditional love binds two or more souls together eternally. There is nothing that can destroy it. Outside

stressors only strengthen unconditional love. Remember, this is what a soul is, pure unadulterated love. It is the same love that comprises God. It is the same knowing. It is the same level of concern. Unconditional love between soul-dominant ones is at the highest level of creativity. Unconditional love emanating from a soul-dominant one to a soul-emergent one is like a mother taking care of her young. It is nurturing and restorative. Ego-dominant relationships are recipes for disaster as there is no creativity there. It is just individuals making it up as they go, while looking out for number one first and foremost. Relationships empowered by soul are happening now and will be the new way moving forward.

Letting Go

11. What should we let go of? Let go of everything that enslaves you, everything that holds you back from freedom. Start with your human identity because what you are is not wholly human. You are just trying it on for size. You are just visiting the earth for a period of time. Enjoy it. Let it show you the ropes. Let it challenge you, but don't let it fool you into believing you are something you are not. Let go of control. You have very little, and what you do have is in your response or reaction to whatever life throws your way. Life wants to give your soul every opportunity to grow, by helping the character to choose love over fear. Let it. Let go of judgment and be honest in all things, brutally honest. There isn't anything that anyone has done that you haven't at least entertained the thought of, so get real and love everyone unconditionally. This is the real reason why you are here.

Living a Life of Love

12. This is your life's purpose. Can you love the things that are easy to love and those that are not? If you can't love something or someone, can you

wipe the slate clean and get back on track? You see, love is the track. If you aren't on it, you have derailed and need to get back on the track. It is both that simplistic and that complex. If you are in sync with love, you are simply Being. You will know when a response is being asked of you. And if it isn't, you are simply to model being love for all to see. No cares or worries, just trust in your own soul and in its power to inform you and keep you safe. Your soul wants you to trust it until the day comes when that is no longer necessary because you have fully merged with it. It will no longer be a separate thing or a separate part of you.

Miracles

13. What is a miracle? It is a change in perception from fear to love. In other words, it is any time you listen to your soul over the voice of the ego. You have just spent a year exploring your own ego and a second year exploring your own soul. With all of this knowledge and insight about very specific topics, you are more equipped to understand your own inner workings. You can now more easily choose love and, therefore, create a miracle. Miracles are like raindrops during a drought. They have the potential to soak the parched ground that has been so thirsty for them. One miracle can lead to another, which leads to another, which eventually leads to an entirely new way of being. Love will open your eyes and lead you to a greater understanding of yourself and your true identity as an aspect of God. You are a soul from the God collective of love energy.

Chapter Ten

Epilogue

1. Why was this book written? It was written as a gift to every man, woman, and child to help them understand different parts of themselves: the ego and the soul. It was written to help individuals finally see that the ego is connected to nothing, and that the soul is connected to everything. The soul network forms a web that is God. This is the goal of *Soul in the Driver's Seat: A Course in Miracles for Today.* I want you to awaken to the reality that you are part of God and not separate from it, although the ego is designed to tell you otherwise. Knowing about the voices of the ego and the soul will help you make better, more informed decisions, more aware decisions. All you really have to do is ask which voice is speaking, and whether it is coming from a place of unconditional love. This is how you will know in your heart that you are on track and doing the right thing. This is how you will know that you are in alignment with God and all that is good and wholesome in the world. Use this book as a reference tool when you have completed your two-year study of yourself. There will then be higher level materials that I, and other colleagues of mine, have channeled to support you in living as a free soul in the world. These will make themselves known to you when you are ready to find them. At this point, I raise my glass to you in celebration of your willingness to receive what has been very obscure and secretive information. The veil has been lifted.

2. Blessed be, Jesus.

Soul in the Driver's Seat
A Course in Miracles for Today

Volume Two

Chapter One

Introduction

1. There is always more to discover on the spiritual path. The first volume of *Soul in the Driver's Seat: A Course in Miracles for Today* was jam-packed with easily accessible information and two years of exercises. 2. Our goal in *Volume Two* is to take a good look at the collective or societal ego and discover how it works and how it influences the individual ego, making the involved souls' jobs even more difficult. 3. Jesus

Chapter Two

The Mystery Within

1. In this volume of *Soul in the Driver's Seat: A Course in Miracles for Today*, we will look at the power of the collective ego on the earth. But first, let's remind ourselves of what we have accomplished. You have just spent a year learning more about how your own ego works and a second year learning about the voice of your soul and discovering that this voice is your true identity. The soul is the mystery within. It is what we must understand and acknowledge first and foremost as we navigate the murky waters of the collective ego. Let us begin.

2. The soul seeks control of the mind so that its thoughts can reflect the soul's value of unconditional love towards self and others. All judgmental thoughts that stem from the major and minor dilemmas must be cast aside so that only love can pass through the gates. This is an excruciatingly difficult task when you are looking at a single, solitary ego. Because humans are social animals, you are never just looking at a singular entity. Like souls, they too are connected to each other. Unlike souls who are connected to each other and to God by love, egos are connected to each other through thoughts of all types.

3. Any thought that is not unconditionally love-based is either neutral or fear-based. Therefore, the web of human ego-led thought mimics the real reality-based web. This is another effect of the illusion of identity. The egoic web is extremely fragile and is broken in many places. This accounts for all of the difficult and impossible to maintain relationships

that there are here. The soul's job is to reduce and eventually eliminate its character's participation in the human, drama-filled web. Instead, it seeks to bolster the character's belief in, and participation in, the soul's real reality-based web. A web where all are connected eternally to God and to one another. This is easier said than done as characters fall into the traps of the egoic web and hang by thin threads. Simply put, they get consumed by and lost in it.

4. Not only does the soul give life to the human body, but it also must change the body's thought system from me, myself, and I, to we, which is singular commonality in multiplexity. The soul has to convince the character that what it thinks is real is not, and what it thinks is a pipedream is reality. It must convince the character that the human web is largely made-up lies, and that love-based reality is one hundred percent true, one hundred percent of the time. This is something exceedingly rare and has happened so infrequently that one could say it almost never happens. My mother and I knew about our true identities and lived from that knowledge. The world today is vastly different from the one my mother and I lived in, and there are few scattered around today who live as we did.

5. The mystery within is the truth of every man, woman, and child's true identity. It is the soul within. It is God. It is the true self. I've already provided the laundry list of job requirements that it has. If this job were posted on a computer job search site, no one would ever apply for it. Now we will make matters exceedingly more complicated by addressing the elephant in the room, which is the influence the collective false identity has over the individual false identity. Meet the collective ego. It is worse than the wicked witch who was killed by Dorothy's tornado-thrown house. It is that bad.

Chapter Three

The Forbidden Fruit

1. When a singular person or even an entire group of people make decisions from their brains instead of their souls, they have picked fruit from the tree of the knowledge of good and evil. As soon as one piece of fruit is picked, it is replaced by one that is even more appealing yet more dangerous, to both the individual and the group. This is the forbidden fruit.

2. The forbidden fruit is any thought or belief whose source of origin is the brain. The brain only produces products that cement the illusionary false identity into place. These spread like wildfire once they are bought into. If someone tells someone else, or a group of someone elses, about a brain-based thought or belief and it is adopted as truth, then more wildfires are spread. These ideas about the world could be shared in person, online, at a conference, through an article or book, in a podcast, on a TV show, or in a movie. There is always some degree of truth to forbidden fruit. It has to be appealing and it has to taste good.

3. Complete dependence on the brain's thoughts is dependence on perception and half-truths. It is a drunken, illusionary, dreamlike state where you and other yous get to decide what caused one thing to happen, or what may be behind this other thing or that event. The forbidden fruit keeps replacing itself once bought into. There is never an end to thought and perception because its fuel is fear, and fear is

rewarded here. It is the standard. It is the expectation. It is constantly and continually reinforced.

4. Seeing through the eyes of duality has been the only option here. The brain perceives everything as good, bad, or neutral. This is the result of being human to begin with. Eating from the forbidden fruit has been the only choice here. Humans have learned over time to temper their reactions to things they perceive as good or bad, in order to preserve their own mental health. Someone may perceive heroin as good and could quickly develop a drug dependency or experience an overdose. Someone may perceive that shooting someone is a good thing as long as they felt justification in doing so. Those of the religious persuasion have felt in times past that modern music, dancing, and wearing makeup were all bad and would lead someone straight to the depths of hell. So as you can see, seeing through the brain's eyes of duality is in the eyes of the beholder. There is always some consensus but only some.

5. Eating from the forbidden fruit is to be human, and as I've already stated, it has been the only option until now, that is, when education about the soul is becoming available. This book is an example of this type of education which, simply put, promotes listening to the inner voice of the soul instead of the ego's voice of judgment and duality. Because the ego is not a solitary system, it joins with others to create joint systems that either promote or fight other joint systems, in the name of what is right and what is wrong. Along with this promotion or opposition is the precious "identity card." The promise is that if a solitary ego will join this cause or that cause, they will not only have a membership card to carry in their wallet, but a new one or another one to wear and show off to others. Someone could affirm their allegiance or revulsion to a cause or set of beliefs and gain new alliances and new enemies.

6. In summary, eating the forbidden fruit from the tree of the knowledge of good and evil is a given, as it becomes part of the consumer's identity.

Humans are always eating it and encouraging others to eat of it. It is about what's bad, what's good, what's wrong, what's right. It's about who is evil and who is a victim. It's about fighting this and fighting for this. There will never be an end to the varieties of this fruit, as they change with the times. But if you look carefully, each seemingly new piece is just the same old, same old, wrapped up in a new package.

7. Remember, the soul's main objective is to convince the character to stop listening exclusively to the voice of the ego. This is complicated when you realize that the ego's voice is not only an internal one. It is also an external one because the human is a social animal. In fact, this external voice is the louder of the two. The external ego is, in and of itself, a dual system. The internal ego likes and agrees with one part of it and does not like or approve of the other part of it. There are three main egos: an internal sense of self, an externally bought-into sense of self, and an externally rejected sense of self.

8. The forbidden fruit is a poison that has wreaked havoc in society since the beginning and continues to do so to this day. All true healing comes when the character stops listening to both its own egoic voice and the one in the collective. The soul needs the character to stop listening to the voices of separation and independence from the soul. This is all quite insane, after you finally realize that you are a soul and always have been all along.

9. Love, true unadulterated, unconditional love, is the only antidote for the ego's poison. Although the ego has had, and continues to have, the upper hand in this world, individual and collective identification with soul is the only way out of enslavement and towards true freedom, towards the promised land. Eating from the forbidden fruit only produced tyranny. It was a trick of false advertising of epic proportions.

Chapter Four

Treacherous Waters

1. The landscape of the beautiful earth is marred by the treacherous ego, both individually and collectively. They have joined forces against one another and against their common enemy: the soul. The ego is threatened by the soul and yet it doesn't really know what the soul is. It knows that the soul is alien and doesn't speak its language. The language of the soul is foreign to the ego as unconditional love cannot be processed by fear. The stronger some souls have become, and the stronger the soul network has become, the more irrational the collective ego has become.

2. The ego can seldom tolerate being corrected by other egos. It never tolerates correction from a soul. Remember what a miracle is. It is a change in perception from fear to love. It is direct movement away from the ego towards the soul, the thing the ego fears and is unable to understand. Egos have many common enemies, but the one that is front and center is that which it can't define and master: the soul.

3. The collective ego only wants fear-based thinking and nothing else. It rewards this and it punishes nonconformity to this low-level standard. It is only fair at this point for a full disclosure, after you have spent two years getting to know your own false sense of self and your true self that is in alignment to love and not in opposition to it. The full disclosure is this. You will not be supported by either your own ego or the collective ego once you start to listen to and follow up with your soul. You will be cast out, shunned, and deemed unworthy. The

world of ego has no place for you. It has no place for the realness of the soul. It has no place for true love.

4. What is the definition of a miracle worker? It is a human who lives as a soul, as a free spirit, in a world of conformity to the confines of the individual and the collective ego. It is someone who goes against the stream, simply put. It is someone who thinks in alignment with unconditional love and not fear. It is not someone who is against the ego and fearful thinking per se, but it is someone who sees it for what it is and doesn't buy into it. A miracle worker sees others as themselves, not less than or better than, but the same. They, too, are souls struggling to be heard in treacherous waters.

Chapter Five

The Vast Conspiracy

1. The collective ego is what defined the term *normal*. The collective ego has always been driven by rich and powerful individual egos, who rule through power and intimidation. This is the unbroken rule that continues to this day. Individual egos are afraid to not comply. They have seen what happens to others when they even try. In more open societies, the penalties for nonconformity are less severe, but they still do their job of discouraging dissent. I'm not talking about issues of the day as much as I'm talking about general expectations for what is considered normal.

2. Who gets to decide what is normal and what is acceptable? Where is the freedom in these concepts? Why would an individual have to comply with established or implied norms in order to be acceptable? Why would an individual have to be acceptable in order to be liked? The collective ego has many smaller collective egos underneath its umbrella, and all of them expect some type of buy-in in order to avoid punishment. Explicit rules of conduct are where social contracts or laws are created and enforced for the benefit of the group. Where is love in all of this?

3. What I'm about to say may not make sense initially but will after careful contemplation. The human brain is so powerful that it has created its own alternative reality (without goggles) that is its reality. Misinformation, misunderstanding, and fear of what could very well happen to someone if they dare to question why it is there to begin with, all keep the illusion of being human firmly in place. It isn't that you aren't human but that

you aren't wholly human that has been kept from you. This, along with all of the false beliefs and restrictions about being human, has created the vast conspiracy.

4. The vast conspiracy is an aspect of the false set of beliefs I have so often referred to as an illusion. The vast conspiracy is the enforcer behind the illusion. It is the muscle of the illusion. It is the one you wouldn't want to meet in a dark alley. It is what will punish your noncompliance. It simply states that those who offend it for whatever reason will pay in one way or another. How can an illusion have an element that serves as a punisher, you may ask? This question is easy to answer. Every time a singular ego reacts either positively or negatively to something in the collective ego, they create a strengthened fear-based energy. While this, too, is illusionary, it is a very real thing to contend with, here in this alternatively real human world.

5. The dogma of the vast conspiracy is that no singular ego within the illusion be allowed to leave it. Everything it does is designed to accomplish this objective, and it has been amazingly successful throughout human history. Very, very few individuals have been able to accomplish the gargantuan task of discovering they have a soul and then functionally operating as one in their day-to-day life as John or Mary Smith. The vast conspiracy has provided everything necessary to prevent this from happening. Just as egos think they are real and that the body itself represents them, the collective ego thinks it is real and that the vast conspiracy of societies themselves represents it.

Chapter Six

Evil Incarnate

1. I do not want us to get caught up in semantics here in this section. In the original *A Course in Miracles* I said that there was no such thing as evil. If evil is inspired by or caused by the influence of a Satan-type of figure or by demons, then this is true because these types of beings only exist in horror novels and movies. I must set the record straight now while I have this great opportunity to do so. This is because readers of the original text felt that something was amiss with their own perception by seeing evil acts of all types in the world, or at least trying to see evil acts as nothing more than mistakes. This was certainly not my intention and if I caused confusion with anyone, I sincerely apologize. Now, let us continue.

2. Let's be clear. In today's world and in the world since the beginning of time, individual and collective egos have taken it upon themselves to create catastrophically devastating loveless acts that have altered, cut short, or ended the lives of countless individuals. I don't care what you call them, but what I do care about is how you understand them. I don't need to create a list of loveless acts here. Everyone knows what we are referring to. Human nature itself is to blame. Anger and hatred are to blame. The competitive nature of humans is to blame. Jealousy and rage are to blame. Faulty relationships are to blame. The belief in a lack of resources is to blame. The inability to process trauma and grief is to blame. If you want to call the behavior of all of these elements evil,

then fine, go right ahead, but do not exclude yourself from the label you are using. Maybe your brother-in-law shot your sister and abused his children. But admit it now, there have been times when you were troubled enough to do something similar, as far as causing harm is concerned. Thinking about doing harm may not be as bad as actually doing harm, but it isn't innocent either. Let's be honest here. The problem with the word *evil* is that it shouldn't just apply to the ones who pulled the trigger. If one is evil, then so is everyone, and I know this isn't the case. How can a soul aspect of God be evil?

3. In summary, terrible and frightening things happen in your world every second of every day. These are loveless reactions. They are against all that is whole and good. They all go against the sway of the soul's voice. They are against life itself. Sometimes it's a lone actor who has been influenced by the more negative aspects of the collective ego, or maybe it is a collective ego itself. More inhumane acts are caused in the name of religion or nationalism than for any other reason. So whether we call loveless and harmful acts evil or not, isn't as important as knowing that they are frequent and by-products of the singular or collective ego. Egos are potentially dangerous at best and actually dangerous at worst.

Chapter Seven

Rational Thought vs. Irrational Thought

1. A singular ego can be considered normal and healthy. It can also be wounded by countless things that cause it to question its self-worth. It can become bitter and angry and self-isolate or find collective egos for those who are bitter and angry to bond with. It can self-medicate with drugs and alcohol. It can become diagnosed with mental illness and think of itself as a labeled pathogen. It can see its worth in how much status it has and how much money it makes. It can be so externally focused that it depends solely on others to befriend and like it. Now that I've described most everyone you know, including you, let's take a good look at how egos actually think. How much of their thinking is rational vs. how much of it is irrational?

2. If the ego causes you to think you are something you aren't and causes you to think you're alone in the world and have to fend for yourself, then I could argue, and did argue in the original *A Course in Miracles*, that all human thought is irrational and not based in reality. Now that I'm adding meat to the bones with this new edition that is much more subtle in its explanations of things, I can say that much of human thought is perfectly understandable in the context of the alternative reality it functions within. It is irrationally rational.

3. Most egos find ways to function in the world so that they can obtain what they need and want. Needing food, shelter, and transportation, and recognizing these needs, are rationally oriented thoughts. Just

needing them in order to survive, without any other purpose, is irrational. Not knowing the truth about one's identity is the cause of all irrational thought. Although this isn't anyone's fault, the natural process of discovering your true identity as a soul of God, has been purposefully made much more difficult by the collective ego. In fact, it has sealed the deal and made a natural discovery almost impossible.

4. The collective ego umbrella of countless collective egos is the real culprit in promoting false narratives and ensuring that they are cemented in place so that the truth of what is really transpiring here cannot possibly get out. If you want to call this evil incarnate go right ahead. I don't mind if you call artificial systems evil. By design, their ideology is quite irrational on top of their diabolical nature. Just keep individuals out of the box of evil please. Individual egos formed the collective ego out of a fearful desire to understand themselves and the world, which is an innocent intent. When false ideas spread and become even more identities, irrational thought gets the upper hand. And that is precisely what has happened here.

Chapter Eight

Epilogue

1. The situation on the earth is so complicated. Writing a book about how humans function in actuality, and how they could function in potential, can't be complete without looking at the social component. No one is here by themselves, so we have to look at the relationships between the individual and the group. We need to look at how the group influences the individual and how a lucky few individuals stroke their own egos by influencing the group. Being aware of this connection is paramount to being willing to leave relationships that are codependent and not whole (unholy) in order to move towards creating soulful relationships that are whole (holy) in nature. The pathogens that permeate the landscape have infected and affected all human relationships since the very beginning. A soul-dominant life must see these relationships for what they are. This second volume of *Soul in the Driver's Seat: A Course in Miracles for Today* is my attempt to help you to see with clarity. It is my attempt to help you to shine a light on the world and see it for what it is and what it can become.

Soul in the Driver's Seat
A Course in Miracles for Today

Volume Three

Chapter One

Introduction to the Mirror Exercises

1. All parts of *Soul in the Driver's Seat: A Course in Miracles for Today* are highly important, even critically important, but this next part is the most crucial part. Welcome to the "Mirror Exercises – A Look in the Mirror." If you have spent a year getting more familiar with the workings of your own ego and a second year doing the same with your True Self, your soul, then you are ready for a third tool. The Mirror Exercises are tools for the maintenance of soul dominance. Just because you have deeply explored both your ego and your soul, it doesn't mean that your ego isn't going to creep in and try to drag you back into illusionary thinking once again. No, no. The ego is consistent, and it will see itself as not doing its job if it isn't trying to get your attention on a moment-to-moment basis. The Mirror Exercises, simply put, are specifically designed for maintenance of living in reality. Awakenings from the illusionary identity are fragile and must be supported. Reading spiritual books repeatedly may just result in burnout. We need something else. There will be a total of twenty-four Mirror Exercises, one per month for two years. Each one can be practiced daily or at least weekly for that particular month. When a new month begins, move on to the next exercise. Upon completion of both years, these exercises may be repeated as the soul prompts.

Chapter Two

Mirror Exercises: A Look in the Mirror
Year One

January: Judgment

1. This month, I would like you to set aside five minutes each day for this exercise. It can be in the morning, during the afternoon, or in the evening. Go through the day's events in your own life's experience and the things you have observed firsthand in your inner circle and from a distance through media of all types.

2. Ask yourself these three questions:

    1. Did I shame myself for any action or thought today?
    2. Did I shame someone else for any action or expressed thought today?
    3. If the answer to either the first or second question is yes, release this judgment and see yourself and others as whole works-in-progress, where mistakes of all types are expected as the soul is growing.

3. End each session this month with this affirmation:

    I Am whole. I Am progressing in my unity with the creative force.

I Am allowed all of the time I need on this journey. My mistakes are learning tools and nothing more.

February: The Body

1. Imagine for a moment that you didn't have a body. There would be nothing to clean, nothing to feed, nothing to dress, nothing to use to impress anyone. This is your assignment this month. I want you to leave your body through the Holy Instant at least three times a day for as long as possible each time.

2. Then, when you return to body consciousness, ask yourself these three questions:

1. How can I be contained in a body without my body dictating to me what the terms are?

2. How can my body reflect my True Self and not my surface self?

3. How can I practice presence instead of (strictly) image with my body?

3. End each session this month with this affirmation:

I Am not a body, but over time, my body can reflect who I Am becoming on the inside.

March: Characters

1. There isn't a director on the world stage yelling "cut" and then insisting that you play your character with more of this and less of that. No, you are the only one who gets to decide how you play your character. You can play it from a place of soul and unconditional love, or you can play it from a place of ego and everything that is not unconditional love, which is fear. Only you decide which way you will play your assigned character. Will it be your surface self, or will it be your True Self?

2. This month, set aside ten to fifteen minutes each day to focus on your character, which includes your name, family history, personal history, likes, dislikes, passions, hobbies, occupation(s), and relationships. Ask yourself these three questions:

1. Am I free enough to let go of my own expectations for how I play my character?
2. Am I free enough to detach from the expectations of others in relation to how I play my character?
3. Am I allowing my soul to influence how I play my character?

3. End your daily session this month with this affirmation:

I have always felt compelled to play my character according to a set of expectations. My soul begs to differ.

April: Role-Playing

1. You, the character, have played, are playing, and will play numerous starring and supportive roles during your lifetime. Some of these roles were assigned to you and some of them were assigned to you by you. Your family role growing up was assigned to you. But because you chose to be a nurse that role was self-assigned, as was the role of wife or husband if you decided to marry. As we've already explored in last month's topic, only you decide how you play your roles. Do you feel free to play them with soul, or do you feel typecast by the expectations of others and by your own conditioned expectations?

2. Please set aside a fifteen-minute period this month to ask yourself these three questions:

1. How have I played my roles in the past? Look at the childhood years, the teenage years, young adulthood, and continue decade by decade. If some roles bring discomfort, you will know that there is something there to be released and healed.

2. How am I playing my roles now?

3. Since allowing myself to experience *Soul in the Driver's Seat*, how have my roles been played with more unconditional love?

3. After each session, repeat this affirmation:

I choose to play all of my roles with more compassion, more concern for others, more love and less rigidity, and less of me, myself, and I.

May: Character Assassination

1. Character assassination results when the individual or collective ego compares itself to others and finds them lacking in comparison. They simply don't measure up and deserve to be whittled down to size. They don't do the right things and do all of the wrong things instead. They must be punished in semi-private or public forums. It is the self-righteous ego who has been given this job and appointed lord and master over those who fail to impress the ones who need to be impressed. They are the judge, jury, and executioner.

2. This month, set aside fifteen minutes each day to ask yourself these three questions:

1. Have I verbally, or in a written fashion, made someone I know or someone in the public eye the target of any type of criticism or scorn?
2. Can I listen to my soul to understand the behavior of myself and others?
3. Can I see myself in the ones I have criticized?

3. End each session with this affirmation:

We are all here, in this time and space, to grow in the ways of love and forgiveness. Every time I participate in character assassination, I block these miracles from happening.

June: Feelings

1. Feelings are like thermometers. They can let you know what is going on with the ego or the soul or, rarely, both. There are those strange days when the soul's perspective is agreed to by the ego or vice versa. Surface feelings arise from your own thoughts or thoughts from the collective. These include feeling happy and joyous when things are going well, to feeling sad and depressed when they aren't, and everything in between. The soul's range of feelings isn't as vast. Its deeply felt feelings transcend thought and are always loving responses. It, too, feels pain and sadness, but it is from a deeper perspective that is below the level of thought. How do you know which is which? Ask yourself if it is a response or a reaction. Are you happy that your team won the big game? That's an example of an ego reaction. Are you sad about a specific situation? You could be sad about thoughts pertaining to the situation or you could be feeling a deep sense of loss. My advice is to be in touch with all of your feelings, no matter where they come from. Over time, you will be able to sort them out more easily and be at peace with them.

2. There are no specific exercises this month, but I do recommend setting aside time each day to process your feelings about everything. This will be a very healthy habit to maintain.

July: The Holy Instant

1. The Holy Instant is yours whenever you want to leave the illusionary reality of separation for the true reality of unity with all and with God. It is when you leave time momentarily and embrace knowing that you are a soul in truth. You are part of God itself.

2. Three times per day this month, take time to feel yourself change from a heavy presence of matter to a light presence of light energy. Find your portal of entry. It may be your heart area or your head space. Envision yourself opening a door into the unseen world, and when you do, your entire being is awash with divine light and energy. Hold this frequency for as long as possible. Make yourself comfortable because this way of being is your new home. You are a light being now.

August: Your Relationship with the Unknown

1. Before you became known you were unknown, and after you are known you will be unknown once again. The world of potential energy is a world that supports the world of fluidity, where thought becomes form and matter of all types takes shape. If energy leaves form, where does it go? Does it vanish or does it serve other purposes in the grand scheme

of things?

2. Once a day this month, hold the Holy Instant for as long as possible. Let yourself discover more about the world you left partially and the same one you will return to fully one day. How can it support you in this dimension? What messages does it want to convey? Most importantly, how can you be a representative of it as a soul-dominant expression?

September: Love

1. Love is something that is hard to pinpoint exactly. You see plenty of examples in your world of what love is not. You can understand clearly from reading this book that the ego does not operate from a place of unconditional love and does not understand it. But what exactly is it, and what forms does it take? Love is the concern for the safety and welfare of all. Love is supportive of the soul within all. Love allows the soul to do its job with its character, without external judgment of said character – judgment which could complicate things and make the soul's job harder.

2. Let me ask you a question. If love always exists in potential or manifests in the form of doing, does this mean that it is always nice? Let me put it this way. Love is usually very nice, kind, and considerate, yes, but not always. Love is the strongest untapped power in the world. Love can be very stern and intolerant of the nonsensical rubbish that comes out of characters' mouths. Love isn't wishy-washy and isn't afraid to speak its mind. Fear is the thing that is afraid to speak its mind.

3. This month, focus on Love during a daily session. Review your

relationships in all environments in which you operate and ask yourself if fear or love is in the relationship. If both are present, which one is dominant? What can you do to allow more soul into your relationships?

October: Grief

1. Everyone you know and everyone you don't know carries around at least some grief and very possibly large amounts of it. The one thing that everyone has in common is that no one has the skills to deal with grief. You can try to bury it by forgetting about it. Or you can drink and smoke yourself to an untimely death with the nervous energy that comes from it. Grief comes from loss of all types. It comes from experiencing the trauma of both ordinary life events and extraordinary ones. You can lash out at others with your grief, or you can lash out at yourself with it. It is very important for soul-dominant individuals to keep this weed out of their gardens because it spreads like wildfire and makes soul growth next to impossible. Failure to keep grief neutralized could result in ego dominance once again, as thoughts about blame take center stage.

2. This month, dedicate time twice a day to look for acceptance of old and current events in your life. Signs of accepting and being at peace with life's difficult events are good indicators that there isn't any blame and shame there. But what if there is blame and shame? Accept that, too, but be willing to let it go when you're ready. Try to look at everything from a place of neutrality and see all sides of every issue, even the ones that bring you pain.

November: Acceptance

1. We touched on acceptance last month as an antidote to grief. Not getting upset over spilled milk falls in this category. Not getting upset when things don't go the way you wanted them to, falls in this category. Understanding that people create harm when they didn't have to, falls in this category. Understanding that life is messy, oftentimes unnecessarily so, falls in this category. Acceptance is based on your new knowledge about souls and how they work and what they are up against.

2. This month, continue to look for grief, continue to look for attachments to desired outcomes, and continue to look for acceptance of bad things that happened to good people.

December: Forgiveness

1. Forgiveness is essential in this world because the ego does actively place blame for its own actions as well as for the actions or inactions of others. If the ego didn't blame itself or anyone else, then forgiveness wouldn't be necessary. Forgiveness is necessary, however, if you are to be happy. True happiness comes from freedom of all types, most importantly freedom from condemnation.

2. Since this is the last month in Year One's exercises, please spend a solid fifteen-minute session each day in deep meditation. Ask your soul to show you any character or situation from the past or present that you still hold hard feelings about. Bless them and let them go. Do not carry them around with you any longer. What did blaming them show you about yourself? Even if you don't know the answer to this question, let them go.

3. Take a good look at your relationships with those you have blamed in the past. Did the relationship end? And if it didn't, are there still hard feelings that are present? If so, these are indicators that more forgiveness work is in order.

4. What things do you blame yourself for? How can you replace self-blame with unconditional love?

Chapter Three

Mirror Exercises: A Look in the Mirror
Year Two

January: Patience

1. Year Two's set of monthly maintenance exercises will be less structured than Year One's. These exercises are minimal and are meant to be celebratory in nature. Let's celebrate how far you have come in becoming soul dominant and in staying that way.

2. This month, please honor your Self as soul by acknowledging your own patience. Each day, reflect on times in the past and in the present when you have been patient with others and with yourself. Patience leads to less condemnation and less need for forgiveness, so it is a very valuable part of the Gift of Wisdom package.

February: Consideration for the Body

1. This month, we honor the body and how far it has taken you on the spiritual journey. It isn't your identity. But while it is a shed identity, discarded and outgrown, still it serves. It never said it was you to begin with. That was the ego talking and playing games. This month, honor your soul's vehicle. Honor it for what it is, without judgment. It is not too short, too tall, too skinny, or too fat. It is not a disease or a pathogen. It is, and always has been, the perfect vehicle for you to use as you're learning and growing. It looks stern when it needs to, and it looks happy when you let it. Listen to it and discover what it needs from you as far as movement and nutrition are concerned. Its needs are minimal. Just honor your body by letting it be what it wants to be, a reflection of your soul.

March: Gratitude

1. Instead of focusing your attention on things and external situations to be grateful for, do the opposite. This month, be grateful for all of the times your soul has grown. Simply put, be grateful for all of the hard times. These produced soul growth, more of the real you. Look back on your life's difficult times during a daily session of reflection.

What was your soul saying? How was your ego resisting the soul's messages? If difficult circumstances were to revisit you, how can following your soul's guidance result in less internal turmoil and more peace and tranquility?

April: Awareness

1. Awareness means to see the true content of any situation. It is to see what lies beneath the external form. During each daily session this month, let your soul show you the hidden content of anything you inquire about. Ask what is really happening in this situation or that situation. What is really transpiring with this character or that character? Clear your mind and be ready to feel insight from your heart.

May: Serenity

1. The soul is serene, and as you identify with it more and more, this internal state of peace will be yours to own and operate from. Serenity can be yours in the middle of a battlefield. It can be yours in the middle of any kind of chaos. Claim your serenity this month. Each day, set aside time to separate yourself from the noise in your head and be at one with silence.

June: Peace

1. Peace and serenity go hand in hand. Serenity is internal and peace is external. This month, reflect on whether you have peace in your life experience. Is there quiet? If so, this is a good indicator. Is the communication from others purposeful? Or is it constant babbling about this, that, or the other? Are you inundated with violent imagery from screens? If so, take control and place firm limits on what is allowed in your home. If you live with others, let them know what is acceptable in the form of language and behavior. Everything should support peace.

July: Enjoyment

1. This month, focus on enjoyment. Try to enjoy everything you do and experience, and if you can't, try to enjoy some little thing about it. This month, be reminded not to take things too seriously. There is purpose in human life. But maybe the ultimate purpose is that human life is to be savored and enjoyed. Whatever life is sending your way, find the sweet spot. This is one of your soul's objectives, to get you, as the character, to loosen up a bit and not be so serious. Enjoy your daily walk, looking at an upcoming due date on a bill, or unclogging the toilet. Enjoy it all.

August: Solitude

1. Soul-dominant individuals are more comfortable being by themselves. They don't live or die by social contact the way that ego-dominant individuals do. The reason for this is that it is difficult being around the egos of others for more than short periods of time or in large doses if there are multiple egos present. The soul may find that it needs to be selective with social contact because some egos are unpleasant to be around. Solitude is the perfect solution whenever possible. Placing limitations on involvement is important whenever social contact can't be avoided. Certainly, in an employment situation, boundaries will need to be set. The same would apply in family dynamics. If solitude is an aspect of wisdom, then it must be facilitated. This month, take a look at your need for solitude and how you can make room for it.

September: Togetherness

1. Soul-dominant individuals love to be in concert with other soul-dominant individuals. It's when they truly feel connected and can thrive. Being with other heart-minded individuals is very reassuring. Notice that I said heart-minded and not like-minded. Egos find other egos who are like-minded to spend time with. Souls find other souls who are

heart-minded to spend time with. A balance of solitude and togetherness is just what the doctor has ordered for soul-dominant individuals, in a world consumed by ego. If you haven't already done so, reach out or respond to other hearts who want to connect with you on the heart level. This is your suggested assignment for September of Year Two.

October: Wholeness

1. How are you doing with the concept of wholeness? If the old concept of being solely human is a fragmented one that is missing a key ingredient, then the new concept of being a soul having a human experience is a complete one. How do you see yourself? This month, perform a daily check to look for signs of separation and brokenness. Ask your soul to show you ways you can feel unified as both an eternal and a mortal being.

November: Kindness

1. In your world there are acts of kindness, many of them in fact. There are acts of kindness on the surface, where individuals do nice things for one another. These are typically of the I'll scratch your back if you scratch mine variety. Going deeper, there are anonymous altruistic

acts of kindness that are done out of pure love, without any expectations whatsoever. What I want you to focus on this month is yourself. This is "be kind to yourself month," folks. There is to be no self-criticism, no self-blame, and no Monday-morning quarterbacking. With acceptance of all parts of yourself, both ego and soul, comes kindness towards both parts. This month, take yourself out to do something special at least once a week, in honor and respect for the individual that you have become.

December: Wisdom

1. Can you see how wise you have become? Can you see that you have moved away from pure ego identification, and where there used to be no space between ego and your identity, now there is? From this space, you are free to choose between ego and soul in a moment-to-moment basis. You can choose between love and fear, and when you choose love you are creating more space. In this space, you are lessening the ego's power and increasing the soul's power. In other words, you are creating miracles, which is what this entire book has been all about. You are changing your own perception. You are becoming a miracle worker.

Chapter Four

The Calm After the Storm

The Exalted

1. You are the exalted one now. You know more about your surface self now than ever before, while also knowing about your true identity. Knowing makes choosing easier. You don't have to automatically choose the default mechanism anymore. This knowledge that you now have gives you more freedom than you've ever known. You are free to choose between love and fear and are not obligated to choose fear out of ignorance and obligation. You have taken one step out of the abyss after having completed the strange, new *Soul in the Driver's Seat: A Course in Miracles for Today*. Now, you are the exalted one.

The Crown

2. We crown you, as you are truly royalty, walking the earth as a commoner. There is no pomp and circumstance surrounding you. You are simple and yet you are the divine, the awakened, the soul dominant. You are the one who knows. You are a miracle. You are love incarnate. I can list your attributes indefinitely but can summarize them in only one. You are the answer here.

Simplicity

3. The complexity of the ego knows no bounds. It is constantly planning

a seemingly endless number of tasks that it feels compelled to accomplish. Once the list is finished, another one is started, and then another, and another. Past accomplishments from past lists are frequently revisited and evaluated. Which ones weren't up to the standards the ego is always setting for itself and for other egos? These evaluations provide unnecessary stress for all new lists. The soul is nothing like this. It simply doesn't care about the past and isn't involved in evaluating it. As for now, the soul does what it feels called to do, in a peaceful and nonevaluative manner, and in its own timing. Your soul does not provide stress. It is stress free because of its simplicity. This simplicity is free of all judgment and is freeing because of this.

Purpose

4. The ego has no purpose, but it is always searching for one. When it thinks it has found one, it will discard it. If it gets bored with the purpose it has found, or if there aren't enough rewards embedded in it to make it worthwhile, it will search for another one. The soul doesn't have to search for anything. It already knows what its purpose is. The soul's purpose is to express unconditional love in a place that is hostile to it. It is this simple, and it is this difficult. The difficulty is in getting the character to go along with the soul's purpose, by choosing unconditional love more often. This is the great purpose for everyone who is here now, for everyone who has ever been here, or who will ever be here.

Drive

5. The ego has drive. It will plan and even plot out a list of actions that it thinks are necessary to get what it wants. Some egos will never give up, for fear of being considered a quitter or a loser by other egos or even by itself. Sometimes, the ego's drive has to go against everything that seems to have conspired against it, to prevent it from getting what it

wants. You have all heard the stories of the successful authors, musicians, actors, and businesspeople who experienced failure and rejection for a long period, before success finally found them. What about the soul? Does it have drive? The short answer is yes, it certainly does. It has drive to encourage its character to choose unconditional love over fear. The difference is that the soul isn't invested in particular outcomes. It knows that love takes different forms. The ego is invested in particular forms, but the soul allows love to work its magic as it may.

Determination

6. Drive only takes the ego or the soul so far in life. It must be paired with determination to assure success when the chips are down, and there will always be times when this happens. Determination is the ability to pick up the broken pieces and keep going. Most egos experience determination to accomplish a set goal, but the soul's determination isn't connected to an ego-led goal. It is only connected to the soul's entire purpose, which is to encourage the character to choose unconditional love over fear. Souls never give up, even after being unsuccessful for most of a seventy-five-year lifespan. Some souls are assigned very difficult characters, but that doesn't stop them from trying or from waiting it out. Some characters aren't even aware of their own souls until they are in hospice care on their deathbed. This is how determined souls are. They will wait that long.

Perspective

7. The soul's perspective is the realization that it is surrounded by other souls. Yes, the characters can, in fact, be making it quite difficult for their souls, but the souls knew what they were signing up for. A little resistance here and there, or even a lot of resistance all the time, only makes the soul growth more glorious when the time is right for it to

happen. Compare this perspective with the one of the ego and you will see a huge difference. The ego only sees other egos and the problems they are creating. Or it tries to dance around other egos in order to prevent difficulties from erupting. Choose the perspective of the soul for your own peace of mind. By the way, this topic was known as *separation* in the original *A Course in Miracles*. It has needed some practical updating.

Ways of Being

8. The soul has two ways of being in its simplicity. It can be expressive in its service to all souls, including itself. It can also be receptive and in a state of stillness. Once again, in reference to the original *A Course in Miracles*, this is what giving and receiving are one in truth means. Both action and stillness or inaction, come from the one soul. The one soul that is comprised of all souls, the one soul of unity. The one soul does not experience separation, even though its many parts have many different functions, just as one body has many parts with many different functions that add to the whole. All functions contribute to the whole and each soul can fluctuate between its two ways of being. These ways of being are also known as masculine and feminine, although the lines are becoming more fluid and less defined, as evolution informs creation.

The Gift of Wisdom

9. It is the vast wisdom of the soul that has brought you to this point of no return. A point of understanding and acceptance of your human self and equal understanding and acceptance of your divine self. You understand both parts and where their characteristics come from. You understand the dilemmas and know when your ego wants to drag you down into a rabbit hole. You can hear your soul and take the higher road. When you have sided with the ego, you can simply choose again.

You can forgive your mistakes and leave them in the past where they belong. You can choose your soul's messaging so often and so consistently that you will eventually start to see the soul as not just part of you, but as all of you. You will see the soul as all of who you are, and you will step out into the world with the same body but with only love in your heart. The ego's fear and reign of terror will be over. The nightmarish illusion will be over, and reality will have set in. You will see clearly and will bid confusion farewell. This is what your effort in taking this course will have brought you: all of the gifts of wisdom. They are yours now.

The New Order

10. The new order is when you, everyone you know, and everyone you don't know awaken to their soul's existence, its possibilities, and its hidden identity and connections. The true answers to all of humanity's problems have been here all along, the whole time. The ego's resistance has been so great and powerful that it has tricked you into believing complete lies and outright falsehoods, to keep you engaged with it. Now that you know the truth, what will you do? How can you live differently here with love as your guide? How can you be a soul of God and not just a walking, talking puppet? If your answer is that you can't turn back but can only move forward one step at a time, one moment at a time, in love, dignity, and grace, you are part of the new order. Welcome. Let's move forward together.

11. Jesus

Chapter Five

A Clarification of Terms

1. **Soul**: Source energy that starts its journey in seed form and grows throughout lifetimes. It is part of the totality of God and is an eternal representation of unconditional love towards itself and towards others.

2. **Ego**: A self-serving, artificial, fear-based operating system for the body, the forms of which are both singular as well as collective, based entirely on perception and ideas.

3. **The Body**: A vehicle for soul development in truth. In the alternative reality of human life, it is the representation of the ego that physically houses the false concepts of "me, myself, and I."

4. **The World**: The natural world and all of its wonders are part of the totality that is God, as are souls. The human world reflects separation and division, as it is a reflected mirror image of the ego.

5. **Illusion**: Inaccurate perception that results in the belief that the body and the brain's ideas represent oneself in the world.

6. **Love**: The creative force in this and all universes.

7. **Fear**: The destructive force in this and all universes.

8. **Evil**: When the fear of love rules over and permeates the landscape.

9. **Dilemma**: The friction caused by an ego-based way of thinking and a soul-based way of thinking.

10. **Character**: Exterior you, personality, personal history, likes, dislikes, skills, strengths, and weaknesses. Temporary and subject to change.

11. **The True Self**: The soul, eternal and never changing except in potency and strength.

12. **Holy Instant**: A remembrance of wholeness between the True Self and all that is.

13. **Collective Ego**: An umbrella term that includes group identities that are for and against ideas, policies, things, and other groups.

14. **Pathogen**: All false ideas and beliefs that spread like a virus, including, but not limited to, identity.

15. **Identity**: Identity can be entirely false, entirely true (rarely), or somewhere in between.

Soul in the Driver's Seat
A Course in Miracles for Today

Soul Companion

Chapter One
Introduction

1. This is Jesus once again and I have returned to put some finishing touches on my book *Soul in the Driver's Seat: A Course in Miracles for Today*. I will do that by adding one last part to the three volumes that make up *Soul*. This is *Soul Companion* and it is a complementary part. It will discuss new topics that were not specifically addressed in the original parts.

2. This will be the first time that Rick will help to guide the pacing. For the original parts, I set a heavy task mastery schedule due to wanting them to be seen as fast as humanly possible. This time, Rick will meet with me each day but will let me know when he needs a break and for how long. This part will be finished when it is finished. We are eternally grateful to Rick for answering our many becks and calls and now for this last part of *Soul in the Driver's Seat*, he will have the lead voice as far as timing and scheduling are concerned.

3. This new part of *Soul in the Driver's Seat*, called *Soul Companion*, will be a journal for written expression from a unified soul/body/mind vehicle. It will follow the familiar and very successful format seen in the "Steps to Authenticity" and "The Gift of Wisdom." We will follow the same sequence of topics. Each monthly topic of *Soul Companion* will have a narrative, a series of open-ended guided questions for written response, and universal truths that are to be applied to each human experience. There will be one prompt per week.

4. This is the Introduction, Jesus

Chapter Two

Year One

Introduction

1. Year One will focus on the twelve topics of "Steps to Authenticity."

January: Judgment – How Did I Get Here and Why?

February: The Body – Commonly Asked Questions

March: Characters – The Age of Reason's Destruction

April: Role-Playing – Stop the Car! I Want to Get Out!

May: Character Assassination – More Commonly Asked Questions

June: Feelings – Anger and Its Aftermath

July: The Holy Instant – Morality. Is There a Right and Wrong?

August: Your Relationship with the Unknown – Will I Ever Feel Like I Belong Here?

September: Love – The Divine Order of Things Here and Everywhere

October: Grief – This All Sounds Good and Fine, but Is It True?

November: Acceptance – Is Peace All It's Cracked Up to Be?

December: Forgiveness – Why Has This Taken So Long?

2. You may start this journal style workbook any month of the year. Begin with the first week of the current month and apply the prompt to your writings for that week. Carve out time from your schedule to get in touch with your thoughts *and* your feelings about a specified topic. These will primarily be private responses, but you may certainly share them with others in group settings, if you feel prompted to do so. Godspeed.

January: Judgment
How Did I Get Here and Why?

1. What was your life's purpose before you read *Soul in the Driver's Seat*? How many purposes did you have? Did you give them to yourself through free will or did you feel compelled to create purposes for your time and energy? Who was it who tried to influence your choices and who was it or had the final say?

2. Ultimately, it was you who provided at least some amount of consent, but now you are well versed in the fact that it was only the character making these huge life decisions, such as creating and fulfilling purpose.

3. Now that you know who you really are, in truth, your purpose in being here is going to be at a much deeper level than any role you could play or any service you could provide.

4. This section is called "How Did I Get Here and Why?" You got to this place out of either frustration or curiosity or both. Life on the surface loses its attraction at some point. The unlimited amount of rides and trips through the many haunted houses of terror failed to deliver the goods at the crossroads of life, when your soul came knocking. You listened and opened the door. You have completed a full two-year life review, unlike any other, and you have had access to a two-year maintenance program. Now we need to go further. *Soul Companion* is a workbook for driving souls to use their newfound maturity and wisdom in the context of the world scope you have found yourself in.

5. What will living a soulful, soul-focused life provide for you that your ego-based life did not and could not do for you? How will having a soul lifestyle affect those around you?

6. The most crucial piece of information you now carry with you is that your soul is God and God has grown from a tiny seed to a full manifestation. You now have power you didn't have access to before. God is now in your family and your circle of friends. God is in your neighborhood and in your city or town. So, what can God do as you that the character and role-playing form of you, the idea-driven form of you, couldn't do?

7. Week 1: Use your written words to explore how you have experienced racism, either directly or indirectly.

8. Week 2: Use your writing to explore your own attitudes and judgments about those of a different race.

9. Week 3: Write about your own bias about people who are part of organized religion, either the same one you grew up with or one you are less familiar with.

10. Week 4: Write about your experiences, either personally or observed, with the treatment of gays, lesbians, or transgendered people.

11. Remaining Days of the Month: Knowing that judgment takes many forms, use these days to explore a topic of your own choosing, related to judgment.

12. You have just spent an entire month exploring some types of judgment that are very deeply ingrained prejudices. Why now? Because you're finally ready to purge things that you may not have known were there. Before this moment in time, you simply weren't ready to do this. To answer the question, "How did I get here and why?" you must realize that your ego's willingness to allow the soul to take you through this program put you in the position you are in now. But why? Let me ask you this. If soul identification means more freedom and ego identification means more enslavement, then more freedom awaits the deeper into the soul that you get. This is how you were able to journal through these prompts and why you are freer now because of it.

February: The Body
Commonly Asked Questions

1. This section gives readers of Soul's "Steps to Authenticity" an opportunity to explore their own questions about February's focus on the human body through journaling. Remember, instead of right and wrong, we are aiming for more alignment with soul and less with ego. It is never going to be all of one that will be the ultimate goal. It will be mostly soul, mostly heart, with some mind for balance. You are living in the mind's world after all. Those who would attempt to live and function here with one hundred percent soul would have a very hard time functioning in day-to-day life. You can save being at the one hundred percent soul level for when you leave this realm and return to your true home. Until then, let's aim for a nice balance that will be individualized from person to person.

2. Week 1: Reflect on your body image this week. Do you feel that you have to do anything at all to be accepted by others? Do you have to lose weight, become more muscular, eat "better," dress differently or have any type of plastic surgery or cosmetic surgery?

3. Week 2: What if you presented yourself as you are, warts and all? Can you love yourself and your body no matter what anyone else may have to say about it?

4. Week 3: Reflect on terminating a pregnancy. Can you accept that someone may have an unplanned pregnancy and may feel that having a child to be adopted by others, or raising a child themselves, may not be a wise decision that is in their or a child's best interests?

5. Week 4: Souls are never harmed in any way, shape, or form. If one is

prevented from incarnating, they will wait indefinitely. They are asking to be mentored and if a potential mother is not ready to be a mentor, this decision is respected. Reflect.

6. Remaining Days of the Month: This week, explore your feelings about extreme forms of exercise. Does this reflect image or presence?

7. Body image and pregnancy termination are two of the biggest issues that humans face. They wonder what they should do to please themselves and others. They wonder if they would lose friends if they stopped towing the line of expectations.

8. Even concepts of God have caused great amounts of harm to the peace of mind of countless individuals. They wonder if God will think less of them for ending the continued development of a fetus and not wanting to parent or mentor a child at this stage in their lives.

9. As with everything, the answer to these and every question depend on which "you" is asked. The ego may say one thing and the soul may say something entirely different. There is no pat answer. The soul always guides the character with one hundred percent unconditional love and the ego always guides the character with one hundred percent of its convoluted interest in "me, myself, and I." The soul never judges the character for what it does or doesn't do, but the ego is consumed with judgment.

10. In summary, for all questions small and large, that quiet voice deep within will tell you what is right for you in this moment in time. Turn down the noise of the ego and don't respond right away. Keep checking in with the soul until you know, really know, that its advice is the loving response that is best for not only you but everyone around you.

March: Characters
The Age of Reason's Destruction

1. Although many things in the ego-created world have never made sense to anyone, there have always been things that have made sense to most everyone. Social structures and the way things are and should be have provided a basic framework to fall back on when the world at large seems to be falling apart. Certain things seem logical to the ego-led mind, whether they be family dynamics, national identity, or religion. There have always been things that anyone could count on. Stable things, things no one challenged or questioned. Now, everything has changed and will continue to change, even the tried and true. There have been positive and negative changes in family structures and society at large. People desperately want to return to simpler times, but they are out of reach. This month of March, let's take a deep look at your character's reactions and responses to the destruction of all that has made sense.

2. Week 1: How has your character processed all of the social changes in the past several decades? Compare and contrast the reactions you expressed with your soul's responses. Include movements such as those for equal rights for various groups to recent movements such as Black Lives Matter, Make America Great Again, and antiwar efforts in Gaza.

3. Week 2: This week turn the tables. Looking at your responses last week, write about how your character's ego-led reactions to the soulful responses you gave, which included the opposing sides. Can you understand and accept all sides and all viewpoints, even ones that are opposite to the ones that you now hold?

4. Week 3: Now that you are led by your soul and your character is in

alignment with soul or God, how do you process things that happen in the collective that simply don't make any logical sense? This is your chance to write about all of the many injustices in the world, especially those that bother you the most.

5. Week 4: For the last week this month, focus on understanding things in society that you don't like. Through your writing, make a good-hearted effort to understand divisive things and the egos who create divisiveness.

6. Remaining Days of the Month: A soul-led character will not be with this group while opposing the opposition. Through your writing, explore your character's newfound neutrality.

7. Living in a world where there is a good amount of what is considered normalcy, decency, and goodness is one thing, but living in a world where all of this is unraveling is an entirely different scenario. What is good, bad, right, wrong, true, or false? It depends on who you ask or more specifically, which individual or group ego you ask.

8. As a mature soul, you will have access to the answers to all of these questions for whatever context you want to apply them to. Just breathe, find your stillness, and listen to the soul's quiet voice within. Then your character will know how to proceed during external times of ever-increasing turmoil.

April: Role-Playing
Stop the Car! I Want to Get Out!

1. The world does what the world wants to do, largely based on the choices made by its ego-led inhabitants. As stated in the last section, conditions on the earth are becoming very unstable, with answers to basic questions

becoming more and more elusive. Some band together and say one thing, while some say the opposite. This is the perfect recipe for violence and destruction, as you have seen and experienced. I ask you to be a leader during these times and lead by example. Demonstrate what living a soul-based life is like. Show confidence when the ego shows uncertainty. Show positivity when the ego shows negativity. Show peace when the ego shows aggression and hatred. As hard as it may be, show truth when the world seems to be at the brink of self-detonating. Show that there is another way and be that way.

2. Week 1: Concentrate on your family roles this week. Instead of playing a role of sister, brother, mother, or father, focus on serving love from your soul to other souls you have this specific relationship with. Write about what it will be like to discontinue role-playing and begin to serve without all of the expectations that strict role-playing entails.

3. Week 2: Express your feelings through the written word about how you feel when other people in your life are strictly role-playing, and not serving within that role, and therefore not enjoying the freedom that soul expression can provide.

4. Week 3: Return to simpler times, how could movement away from role-playing have provided more peace and joy to not only you, but those around you?

5. Week 4: Knowing that the complexity of these times is likely to worsen in several key ways, write about how you can lighten your load by disengaging from role-playing and embracing service within your assigned roles through soul identification.

6. Remaining Days of the Month: List ways you can be a soulful sister, brother, mother, or father. Include other specific roles you have found yourself in.

7. Being led by soul, source energy, or God is to be the cream of the crop, but here's the reality. While you are the beautiful flower in the garden,

the rest of the garden is rotting and consumed by pests of all types. This is your challenge. Can you stay in pristine condition with bugs and disease all around you? It would be too easy to be a beautiful flower in a beautiful garden. You are to be a beautiful flower in an ugly garden. Be the example. Be the quiet in the storm. Be peaceful during a raging war. Smile when no one else can.

May: Character Assassination
More Commonly Asked Questions

1. Can you live in a society where it is engulfed in self-righteous blame and shame, without participating in it? Someone may blame and shame you, but you won't return the favor. They may even "cancel" you, but you will see the dishonesty because no one here is in a position where they can truly and honestly look down on anyone for any reason. They may think that they themselves have done wrong things in the past, but someone else has done far worse and deserves what is coming to them. This is not the soul's viewpoint at all. The soul only sees innocence, not mistakes, no matter how much harm was caused.

2. Week 1: Use your journaling time this week to explore all of the times your character was accused of wrongdoing. What is the common theme that runs throughout each incident? If you can clearly see that no one had enough information to blame you, then let each character go, one by one. They were each one wrong in their assessments.

3. Week 2: Now, the slate is only half clear. Use your journaling this week to explore all of the times that you blamed others for wrongdoing. Can you see that you did not have enough information for your behavior?

There were things you didn't know and this will always be the case. Let yourself go for all of your character assassinations.

4. Week 3: This week, look at some cases of character assassinations with those in the spotlight. Have you bought into any stories and then participated in punishing or cancelling anyone's movies, TV shows, or music? Even if varying degrees of the stories may or may not have been true, is it your job to make statements in these ways?

5. Week 4: Take the same examples from Week 3 and see each of them in a more positive light. Who are you to judge?

6. Remaining Days of the Month: Speak out when you see any kind of bullying, whether it is in person or online. Write about these incidents in your journal.

7. To live with your soul in the driver's seat is to be responsible. Responsible for what? Responsible for everything the character does and says. It is no use to blame and shame egos and make them feel terrible. It is a waste of time and only spreads around negativity in the illusion. The best course of action is to lead by example and refrain from this behavior altogether. Don't listen to it. Don't repeat it and don't believe a word of it. Characters make mistakes constantly. It's part of the dance between ego and soul and needs to have some level of respect as being part of the divine order of things. By the way, you may be wondering what the questions were for this section. They have to do with how can you see innocence when you know people have committed terrible acts. They may or may not have caused harm to themselves and others, but it is the God within, their soul, that we honor when we do not engage in character assassination. We leave any correction needed to the involved souls. They are the only ones with all the details. They know who, what, when, where, and why.

June: Feelings
Anger and Its Aftermath

1. You each live in a very angry and hostile world. You don't have to look far to witness this. There doesn't seem to be a ceiling to anger. More and more can join their own personal levels of anger together and create a tsunami of anger at individuals, groups, things that went wrong, things that didn't go the way they were supposed to go, and people who dared to stand in the way. Allegedly, God is angry, and this God stands with certain angry groups. They in turn can become self-righteous about their anger since they have aligned themselves with the almighty God that they themselves created. True God energy, divine energy, does not divide, as God is the only thing here in reality. It's just God. That's all. Of course, there's a little more to it, but the truth of God is nothing like what religion has created. In this section, I want each of you to delve into your feelings about all of this anger and rage and violence. It seems that few are unscathed. Let's explore the giant elephant in the room through journaling, in conjunction with the focus for June, which is feelings.

2. Week 1: What makes you angry, even furious? Explore the causes of your own personal rage this week. With each cause, ask yourself this question. Are you really mad at that specific person, thing, or event or were they merely irritants for something else that you're mad at?

3. Week 2: Things and people in this world can irritate you, but can they make you explode in anger? Do they have that much power over you? Where did the anger you carry around with you come from? Were you

taught to bottle up anger instead of finding healthy ways to express it?

4. Week 3: Humans have more in common than they realize. If you just discovered your own pool of anger this month, know that most everyone on the planet is in the same boat. They are ticking time bombs that will destroy others or themselves through passive means. This is where violence and disease come from.

5. Week 4: Honor your feelings, but know that your feelings have to be taken in context. Many feelings are genuine and are to be taken at face value, but they may very well have come from misunderstanding other people and events. Feelings can lead to truth, but only if you continue with your desire for a greater understanding. Elaborate.

6. Remaining Days of the Month: We have focused on anger for your journaling this month. Now, explore other potentially problematic feelings, such as jealousy, feeling deceived, and betrayal. Can souls feel these strong feelings? If so, which one(s)?

7. If you live in an angry world (which you do), does this mean that you also have to be angry? If you live with ego as your guide, the answer is yes. You won't be able to prevent anger from ruining otherwise good life experiences. If you live with soul as your guide, then the answer is no. I'm not saying that you will never get angry. I'm not saying that at all. What I'm saying is that the understanding that your soul will provide will prevent some anger from taking root, holding the character within it. It will also help to dissipate anger that does seep in and give you helpful and positive strategies for dealing with it. There is a solution to all of this anger in the world and it starts with you. Once others see that you aren't foaming at the mouth, they may be interested in learning more about *Soul in the Driver's Seat*.

July: The Holy Instant
Morality. Is There a Right and Wrong?

1. While we're at it, is there a good and a bad? If you've read this far and put in this much effort and work to understand both parts of yourself more intimately, you know there is helpful and there is harmful. You can see this all around you. One problem is that here in this world, it is the ego who has set itself up as the judge, jury, and executioner. As clearly stated in the original *A Course in Miracles*, egos cannot judge anything because they lack the soul's perspective. The soul always promotes love and peace, which are always good and always right one hundred percent of the time. The ego, on the other hand, promotes a small self-agenda that can and often does include harmful acts of all kinds. These are clearly wrong and bad for involved parties simply because love wasn't chosen. In a perfect world, love would always be chosen, but this isn't that type of world, not yet and not for a long time. In this world, we attempt to foster the growth of love over time and in doing so, mistakes are made, ones that affect countless individuals. We view terms like *wrong* and *bad* as temporary mistakes instead of permanent condemnations. I know what you're saying right now. What about those who kill the innocent? What about rapists? These two things are indeed terrible, but because the soul, or God, is involved there are always everlasting opportunities for redemption, for being helpful, and for refraining from harm.

2. Week 1: Look around you this week. What things do you consider to be the result of right thinking? Does everyone agree with your evaluation? If you were to apply the spiritual standard to these items, would each

item be the result of love?

3. Week 2: Look around you this week, once again. What things do you consider to be the result of wrong thinking? Does everyone agree with your evaluation? If you were to apply the spiritual standard to the items on this list, would each item be the result of fear?

4. Week 3: In complete honesty, did you answer the last questions in Week 1 and Week 2 with an emphatic yes? Chances are that your answers were specifically in context with what you know in and about this world. It is difficult to apply spiritual standards here, isn't it? Right, wrong, good, and bad are egoic-based adjectives, nothing more.

5. Week 4: This week, look deep within at times when you yourself or others expressed disapproval over something you did or said, something labeled bad. What do you think caused this behavior? Do the same thing about things you did or said that were good. What caused this behavior? What was the context?

6. Remaining Days of the Month: Write about the spiritual content of good expressions of love. They are one hundred percent altruistic in nature. Did you find any examples that met this standard this month?

7. While you are here in this world, you cannot depend on the ego to lead you in the correct manner for determining the answers to what is right, wrong, good, or bad. The truth is that whatever it tells you is from its viewpoint and is self-serving in nature. There is only one way to know truth as it is and as it applies to this world and that is through the Holy Instant, that moment in time when you leave time for a short while and check in with the all-knowing soul, connected to All That Is. The soul will inform you of love's point of view in all things.

August: Your Relationship with the Unknown
Will I Ever Feel Like I Belong Here?

1. The short answer is no. You are just visiting a foreign land and hopefully find some enjoyment out of observing local customs, language, and culture. Before discovering your soul, you may have at least attempted to find purpose in playing your character, your assigned roles, and the roles you gave yourself because you felt compelled or drawn to do certain things. Maybe you joined a political movement or did some type of volunteer work for a cause you believe in. Maybe you were against something or for something else. Immersing yourself in causes to give your single life purpose and meaning is very important to many egos, but what about you? Does the soul have purpose? Yes, but it looks different than the world's purpose. It is more general than specific. It has nothing to do with identity and everything to do with service for service's sake. When asked why it did this or that, a soul will say "just because I wanted to." There are no expected or even wanted rewards or even acknowledgement. Egos, on the other hand, always expect something in return, even if it is just a sense of belonging.

2. Week 1: We have asked you to live as a soul or free spirit, while having a body and interacting with the locals. Please use your journaling time this week to see if there is any fear of the unseen world, your true home. What are you afraid of and why?

3. Week 2: Does it make sense to you that egos have painted an ugly picture of the spirit world, filled with evil demons of all types? This week, list all of the monstrous villains you believe are in the spirit world and then write next to each one, "my ego told me this to deceive me."

4. Week 3: Even though you are just visiting, explore ways your life can have new purpose in serving humanity.

5. Week 4: The Holy Instant is when you leave the earth's consciousness. When you aren't in the Holy Instant, you are consumed with the sights and sounds of the physical world. Make a list with two columns. On the left, write down ordinary experiences and on the right, explain how the Holy Instant can embellish them.

6. Remaining Days of the Month: Journal ways to maximize your time in your true home. The more you are there, the more at home you will be and the less fear you will have of it.

7. The answer to this question is yes and no. You will not feel connected in standard ways, but you will feel connected in unique and unusual ways. You will feel as if you have your spiritual helpmates on speed dial, while you take care of all of the things that you need to take care of at your job, with your family, or just taking care of yourself. You won't get any accolades from the ego-led characters you interact with, but your soul could care less about what anyone thinks. It is only concerned about what it knows to be true.

September: Love
The Divine Order of Things Here and Everywhere

1. There is order in God's kingdom, underneath the seemingly chaotic and senseless world. While chaos and senselessness are allowed to exist and even flourish, it is the higher order that allows for choices that are less desirable. Choices made from love are supported on the grid and choices made from fear are not supported, but are allowed. These choices

are made within unsupported terrain, a vast land that has not yet been added to the grid. It is and isn't part of the grid because it hasn't been claimed yet. It is like an unincorporated area in your world. It is part of your world but not part of the structure of a city or a town. The goal is always to add unincorporated areas to the Divine grid. This includes all actors who participate in activities or who create things and events not supported by soul. This is the very slow nature of the Divine order.

2. Week 1: This week, make a list of everything that you believe to be love. Include loving acts of all types. When you have exhausted your list and can't think of anything else to add, your list will be finished. Now, cross out the entire list. These are all things that the ego believes love is.

3. Week 2: This week, acknowledge that true love is unconditional and comes from the soul. It doesn't have to be returned; nothing is expected in exchange, and it can take on an infinite number of forms. Few here have ever experienced this kind of love. It is that rare. It would be impossible to make a list, but you can write about ways you are willing to explore love and service in exchange for nothing. This is your topic this week.

4. Week 3: All love, all true love is in service to the great oneSelf, a familial type of collection of an infinite number of souls. Giving and receiving are one in truth. This type of giving will always make you feel good. Will you trust your soul when it asks you to be of service to it?

5. Week 4: True love is fearless and bold. It is completely without fear of any type. Hesitation will be how the ego will stop you from being of service to love. Some personality types for some characters will need to be gently overcome over time so you can be reoriented to love instead of fear.

6. Remaining Days of the Month: Remember to let all of the preconceived ideas from Week 1 go and be open to exploring something that the world knows little about. Write "I Am in service to love now" each of these

remaining days and let this be your new mantra. Also, remember that love does no harm.

7. Love with a small *l* plays a very significant role in the illusionary world of unincorporated characters, relationships, and property. When true, unconditional love from the soul is finally expressed, characters join the grid and then have all of the support that they did not have previously when separation was the name of the game. Aspects of the grid do not play games or grasp at straws. Everything they do has meaning and purpose from the heart. The entirety of the grid supports each and every individual reflection of love with a capital *L*. The temporary nature of form takes on an eternal nature of truth.

October: Grief
This All Sounds Good and Fine, but Is It True?

1. For most of human civilization, getting answers to all of life's myriad of questions has been like grasping at straws. Stories were created and passed down through the generations. There was the angry and vengeful God who judged your every move, and there was the perfect son who had to die for everyone's collective sins. This left you only having to believe in him in order to be forgiven. Of course, there were many other stories that formed many other religions and traditions. Did any of these philosophies answer anyone's questions? Not really. So, here I am, explaining who you are in truth, explaining about the ego, the soul, and the purpose of life. For the vast majority of people, this is the first time that they have heard this information – this very detailed information. I only ask that you don't believe a single word of *Soul in the Driver's*

Seat until you find out for yourself that it is all actually true, and you will. You most certainly will.

2. Week 1: Return to the loss of something, whether that was a job, a relationship, or status of some type. Explore this loss in your journaling this week. Does it still hurt to think about it and feel these feelings again? If so, this wound is still in the healing process and will need more time.

3. Week 2: Going back to the topic you selected last week, have you come to full acceptance of all of the details surrounding the event, as well as the event itself? Knowing that what's done is done and you can't change anything is important. What feelings are coming up for you as you revisit this topic?

4. Week 3: This week, specifically journal about the loss of a loved one through death. Choose one that was especially difficult for you, even if it was decades ago. Write about your relationship with this person. Check in with yourself on your acceptance level and the type of feelings that come up.

5. Week 4: This month as you were revisiting some especially sensitive topics, did any anger come up? This could stem from a lack of control felt or feeling like the situation was unfair and shouldn't have happened. How can your soul help you with new and old situations to help dissolve grief?

6. Remaining Days of the Month: Is there any blame inside of you connected with the difficult situations you explored this month? What steps can you take to move from blame to acceptance? Write a private note for your eyes only to anyone you blame (including yourself) for anything that has made your current life experience more difficult. At the end of the note, set the person free and bless them. Forgive yourself for not understanding and let it go.

7. No one needs to tell you what truth is. No one. Absolutely no one. Not even me. All I can do, all anyone can do, is point you in the direction where truth is. I can then say something, and you will know if it is true

or not. Your soul will always say yes to anything that is true. If it is only partially true, your soul will resonate with the part that is true. Sometimes, your soul will concur that something is true, but your ego will say that it isn't true, and the character will have to wrestle with the two points of view. If truth wins out, then the soul has grown. Its voice becomes louder. The character learns that it is something that it can depend on. The soul will always speak the truth one hundred percent of the time. Sorry, but the ego doesn't come anywhere close to this level of truth. Unfortunately, and even though there may be shreds of truth here and there, the ego only tells you things that are largely not true. Don't believe me. Believe your soul. It is an aspect of God after all.

November: Acceptance
Is Peace All It's Cracked Up to Be?

1. Your world is not peaceful very often. There may be a fragile peace between wars, but is it really peace if it is soaked in dread of more warfare? Is fear a peaceful state? What about all of the noise in the major cities? Being in the country can be peaceful until the loud engine of a jet airplane permeates the sky. What does being peaceful bring you? As a strand of wisdom, it is a gift of the soul to both the character and the world, but why is it important? Is the ego ever peaceful? Sometimes it is and sometimes it isn't, but only outwardly. Just gauging by the incessant self-talk that it participates in, one can see that constantly needing to talk and express its inaccurate views is not something that promotes peace. The soul, on the other hand, only uses targeted and purposeful communication, while simultaneously advocating for peaceful

and nonaggressive behavior. Which one sounds better to you?

2. Week 1: Peace cannot come until there is acceptance. Acceptance must come first. Explore one event in your personal life in the past year where you came to accept that you did not like someone or something and peace came once you did.

3. Week 2: Continue this same prompt, but extend the time frame to five years.

4. Week 3: Continue the same prompt, but extend the time frame to ten years.

5. Week 4: Continue the same prompt, but specifically dedicate time this week to childhood and young adulthood.

6. Remaining Days of the Month: Revisit your feelings of not liking a person or an event without any regard to a specific time frame. As with each week this month, do not judge your feelings. Accept them completely, with one hundred percent unconditional love. Accept that this person or event may have caused great harm to you and yours, and that this may have come from malice or negligence on their part. Embrace whatever it is because it is yours now.

7. Imagine this for just a moment, if you will. Peace can be yours. Peace can be yours no matter what. You can accept that you are in the middle of a battlefield and be peaceful about it. You can choose peace instead of trying to change anyone or anything. You can choose peace instead of seeking revenge. You can choose peace instead of speaking your mind. You can choose peace instead of being involved in conflict. You can walk away. Peace is always an option, and your soul will always advocate for you to choose it. It may be a sign of weakness if you choose it from your ego's point of view, but to the soul it is the highest honor. To be peaceful means that you are listening to God.

December: Forgiveness
Why Has This Taken So Long?

1. Humans have been left to their own devices since the beginning of the experience. They have been free to believe whatever they wanted to believe, about themselves and each other. They have been free to develop language and concepts. They have been free to observe natural phenomena and not see their own place in it. They have been free to get out anger and aggression and feel justified in doing so. They have been free to create roles and to develop societies. They have been free to harness and unleash power. They have been free to develop concepts of a higher power and to see themselves as powerless in relationship to it. All of this is certainly true, but now there is new information that leads to a new choice, a new moment-to-moment choice that isn't really new. It has always existed, but now education is being provided on why it is so important to make these choices from heart, and from soul, and what immediate benefits will come from this choice.

2. Week 1: Reflect this week on all of the times in the past year when you disappointed yourself and fell short of goals that you set for yourself. Forgive yourself for setting unrealistic goals to begin with. The soul doesn't operate as the ego does in setting goals. It is free to create or not create in each moment.

3. Week 2: This week, reflect on the past five years and forgive yourself for times when you said things out of anger and hurt feelings. Forgive those times when you needed others to hear your frustration with them or with certain situations. It's okay. It is likely to happen again. Accept that and move on.

4. Week 3: This week, return to any big events in your current lifetime where you acted out in a way that was uncharacteristic. Maybe there was violence towards others. Maybe there was property damage. Maybe your reputation took a nosedive. Realize for maybe the first time that all of this was the best you could do at the time and then let it go.

5. Week 4: As you move through life, realize that the inner critic (the ego) wants to judge your every move, as do other egos. Simply refuse to let their judgments have any credibility. Always make amends and most importantly, let yourself off the hook.

6. Remaining Days of the Month: Take my advice and lighten your load. You will be happier for it. You are going to make mistakes in life, but you don't have to beat yourself up over it.

7. Simply put, the ego's show is coming to an end. The curtain is slowly falling to the foot of the stage. Souls are taking over one at a time and will revamp society eventually. Love, instead of fear, will be the mantra. It will be heaven on earth, but in the meantime there is much work to be done, and it all starts with you, the reader of this book. You have work to do, starting with the thorough education that *Soul in the Driver's Seat* has provided. Now, you have to apply this education to your actual life and experiences, and this is hard work. Forgiveness is hard work, but that's where your freedom lies. The ego will only give you more of the same old same old, but the soul will take you to places that were previously unimagined.

Conclusion

1. This was a deeper dive into the twelve "Steps to Authenticity." It enabled you to go deeply into your thoughts and feelings about difficult and even painful topics. To live a fearless life, one has to be willing to look at everything, even things they would rather not remember. The twelve "Steps to Authenticity" is a very thorough life review and this one-year journal has helped you to go inside in a much deeper way than just quickly answering a daily question. Now, let's move on to Year Two, "The Gift of Wisdom," shall we?

Chapter Three

Year Two

Introduction

1. Year One addressed the "Steps to Authenticity." Year Two will focus on the "The Gift of Wisdom." As in the first year, each month will have thought-provoking prompts for journaled responses.

2. Year Two will focus on these twelve specific topics.

January: Patience – Wisdom in a Fool's Paradise

February: The Body – I've Been Knocking, but No One's Home

March: Gratitude – Can You Hear Me Now?

April: Awareness – Instant Karma Isn't So Instant

May: Serenity – Time for a Reboot

June: Peace – The Ego Was the First Version of Artificial Intelligence

July: Enjoyment – I Can't Do This Alone; You Have Work to Do

August: Solitude – Now the Real Fun Begins

September: Togetherness – Being a Creator Is Messy Work

October: Wholeness – Divine and Mortal

November: Kindness – Who Knew?

December: Wisdom – Here's a New Pronoun: We

3. You may start Year Two at any month. Begin with the first week of the current month and apply the prompt to your writings for that week. Carve out time from your schedule to get in touch with your thoughts *and* your feelings about the specified topic. These will primarily be

private responses, but you may certainly share them with others in group settings, if you feel prompted to do so. Godspeed.

January: Patience
Wisdom in a Fool's Paradise

1. There aren't many of you around these parts. Typically, wisdom is associated with aging, and the aged are not respected in most of Western society. They are seen as weak and feeble, out of touch. They themselves may not want to think of themselves as old and resist ideas associated with old age. Even being considered wise may be a sign that the road is coming to a dead end. The truth is that all societies would benefit from having wise members at all stages of life. If living a soul-driven life means that one is wise, then surely we need these souls everywhere. They can influence everything from conflict on the schoolyard to making positive collective choices in companies or neighborhoods. Why is wisdom important? Because it comes from the soul. Why is the soul important? Because it is the divine life force. It is God itself.

2. Week 1: I Am you. You are a soul of God. This is your very essence. You are the great life force itself. This week, list all of the things you aren't. These are things you used to think of yourself as, but no longer do.

3. Week 2: As a soul of God, write down all of the benefits of patience, the benefits of waiting, the acceptance of things as they are, things in a messy state of potential.

4. Week 3: As a soul of God, explore the results of the lack of patience in your former life as an individual ego. Take a good, hard look at what listening to your ego gave you.

5. Week 4: As a soul of God, explore the lack of patience in the external world. What are the results? Look far and wide.

6. Remaining Days of the Month: If the world becomes a patient place by and large, what changes, small and large, would you anticipate seeing?

7. You are surrounded by fools, dear one. That's why the earth is considered a fool's paradise. It is inhabited by those who are in different stages of sleep. They range from being in a deep sleep to very drunk to lightly groggy. They can't help it though. It's why I have so often said that they know not what they do. They wouldn't know me or the truth if I stood right in front of them. They only know some very old and very inaccurate stories about someone named Jesus, someone who was born to a virgin, lived a perfect life without sin of any type, and who died a violent death as a martyr. The foolish may believe this story or some version of it or reject it entirely, but to awaken and learn the truth about themselves and me will certainly require a great deal of patience as they adjust. The truth will set them free, but they have to see it and know it first.

February: The Body
I've Been Knocking, but No One's Home

1. There is a cartoon version of me, and this is the only version that is familiar to the world as a whole. In this Homer Simpson type of cartoonish image, I am frozen in time, first as an adult man in his early thirties and then as a supernatural godlike being who is a doorway to God by simply believing it to be so. While some of my teachings were accurately recorded (peace, love, and nonmaterialism), the true message,

that all of my followers need to continue my teachings by living them and by being them, has not been widely brought to fruition. There is another version of Jesus who typically only appears at Christmas time. This is the baby Jesus who is the center of Christmas lore. The truth is that none of these images are true reflections of who I was or who I became or who I Am now. I evolve and grow as do all parts of God. When I knock, figuratively speaking, it is rare to have the door opened and be invited in, as a friend, not as something or someone to be worshipped. All are equal in the eyes of God.

2. Week 1: Your body has been your home all of these years. Reflect back to most of your current lifetime when you thought your body was not just your home, but was literally you. In what ways did it announce to the world that it was you? What qualities did it have? Were there things about it that others disliked about it?

3. Week 2: Now that you know the truth about your body, list all of its attributes, all of its health issues, all of its perceived shortcomings and then say, "I love this about my assigned body. It has helped me to get to the point where I can say and truly mean it: I am not a body. It is only a temporary learning vehicle and that's all."

4. Week 3: This week, list all of the ways that you care for your body. Do you accept things it says to you? Do you rest when it says it needs it? Do you eat when it says that it is hungry, or do you feed it when your mind says you should? Do you respect what it does and does not want to eat? Do you move it when it asks to be gently or vigorously moved?

5. Week 4: This week, try to separate all of your mind's thoughts about your body from the realities of your body. Do you impose all of experts' shoulds on your body, or do you listen to what it wants to tell you?

6. Remaining Days of the Month: Now that you are a free spirit, list all of the many ways that your body can serve you, a soul of God.

7. The many and varied thoughts about Jesus have prevented many from

opening the door to me. Many would not see me if they did happen to open the door. They would see an image frozen in time, a caricature, a poster model for a myriad of differing forms of Christianity. They would see a list of things that they approve of and agree with, or they would see none of these things and quickly close the door. In other words, people think I have something, or achieved something, they will never have or can never do. They want something from a man named Jesus. They think I can give them something that they want: eternal life. They ask for plenty of other things too, before eternal life. In this way, Jesus is like a genie in a bottle. I speak of this Jesus who is worshipped and adored the way that I Am, because it isn't me. It's all fabricated and distorted ideas about me that were never true to begin with. If the real me knocked at someone's door today, unless they have awakened to their own soul's unconditional love, they would tell me to ___ off and slam the door. I wouldn't meet their institutionalized and cemented-in-stone expectations.

March: Gratitude
Can You Hear Me Now?

1. Now that you know all that you do concerning the ego and the soul, it won't be hard for you to understand that people who came to hear me speak during my lifetime had emerging souls. They had awakened enough to understand my messages to a degree. There was a great hunger and thirst for the truth. My disciples had a different level of understanding, a deeper level, a reality for them, not just a hopeful possibility. After I left the earth realm, my teachings became slightly

and sometimes completely distorted. Then they were buried underneath complete falsehoods. We can all thank the collective ego of many in power or who desired power for this. This powerful entity of false identities and false ideas made sure to essentially kill the truth to ensure its own existence. This is where the idea of nailing Jesus to a cross came from. It came from wanting to kill the truth in order to remain in power. The ego wanted to kill the truth, but it didn't succeed because the truth cannot be killed. What it was successful at, however, was to cast the earth into darkness for two thousand plus years, but now the truth is back and is stronger than before. Now you can hear me, the real Jesus.

2. Week 1: The world does practice gratitude or a type of it. The kind of gratitude that is practiced here includes saying "thank you" and "I love you." It is nice. It is polite. People say that they are grateful for money or a new car or a certain person in their life. This isn't what I want you to do this month. This week, focus on nonphysical gifts you are grateful for.

3. Week 2: Let's go even deeper this week and list all of the really difficult times in your current lifetime. For each and every one of these, list one or more things you are grateful that it showed you about yourself.

4. Week 3: This week, list things that you find hard to deal with about others in your life. Next to each entry, dig deep to find the gift for you there. What are you grateful for about things that irritate you? Do you find similar traits or characteristics in yourself?

5. Week 4: Now, go outside each and every day this week and list all of the sights, smells, textures, tastes, and feelings that Gaia or Mother Nature provides for all. Instead of writing that you are thankful for them, find ways to express gratitude to them. They are your helpmates. They remind you of who you really are in truth.

6. Remaining Days of the Month: Take Week 4's prompt and apply it in your everyday life. Find ways to show gratitude for everything, from the

pretty and the easy and the comfortable to the ugly and the hard and the uncomfortable.

7. Not everyone gets or understands this material. Their egos will not let them. The powers that be in the ego-led world will not let them. Everything in the world was established by the mind in order to keep the illusion in place. The human part of the world is entirely man-made. Therefore they needed an alternative savior story that matched their thinking about God and themselves. When Jesus was killed, so was the soul, or so some thought. The soul only waited and now it's time is at hand. It must awaken from a deep sleep so that it can hear me. The soul, or God, is the greatest untapped force in the world. The ego sees it as a threat to its very existence and so be it. Now our voice will be heard, and things will finally change here.

April: Awareness
Instant Karma Isn't So Instant

1. Wrongdoers in your society can get away with things that they do that aren't love-based for long periods of time. Maybe they are good at covering their tracks or maybe an endless line of expensive lawyers do that for them, while they proclaim their innocence and say that they would never even think of doing such a thing. Why is it that some people get caught in their wrongdoing and others get away with it? In your world, people who were misidentified and were not even at the scene of a crime have been imprisoned and even put to death. There is no justice here. Don't get me started on the criminal injustice system. My topic is Karma. It is certainly true that what you put out in the world

comes back to you, whether that be positive or negative. The timing of this is not always what one would hope for. Karma, whether it is of the positive or negative type, has its own timing as it is governed by universal laws and life itself. It has its own mysterious timing, but I can promise you this. Everything one does is noticed and recorded, whether it is an overt action or even a thought. Life finds ways to reward the do-gooders and withhold those same rewards to harm doers at just the right times to promote their soul growth. This may or may not make any sense to anyone who is observing this process play out though. Life is mysterious in this way.

2. Week 1: Being aware is one of the many gifts of wisdom. Being aware of everything going on around you helps you to see which things are calling for love and which things need to be accepted as they are, and which things don't involve you at all. List everything you are aware of in your life and categorize them into one of these categories in your journal.

3. Week 2: This week, do the same exercise but only focus on newsworthy events outside of your realm of influence in your local community, country, or internationally. Categorize them as changeable things that can be sent loving energy in order to do so or things that need to be accepted as they are.

4. Week 3: This week, your journaling is entirely devoted to just you. Focus on your thoughts and feelings exclusively. No sorting or categorization is allowed this week. Just sit with every thought and every feeling. Discover their meaning through your writing. Accept all of your thoughts and feelings that quiet contemplation allows you to be aware of.

5. Week 4: This week, focus on those who are around you. These can be friends, family members, neighbors, or coworkers. Only if you have been explicitly told about them, focus on things that call for love.

6. Remaining Days of the Month: Repeat Week 4's exercise, but this time

focus on things that call for acceptance now that you are explicitly aware of them.

7. People who believe strongly in Karma just want to see that people who mistreat themselves and others will get what's coming to them, some type of corrective action that will teach them to turn their lives around and stop traveling down certain paths. The universe is set up to provide this, so if you worry about when will Karma ever happen, you can stop now. I will let you in on a little secret. Now seems like such a perfect time to do so. Every time you or anyone attaches a judgment to a particular person, group, or situation, you are preventing corrective action from arriving. You are stopping it dead in its tracks. Why, you may ask? This is because you are energy. Everything is energy. If you attach judgment to something, you are attaching energy to it, your energy. Therefore, if Karma is to come, you and everyone else have to detach your energy that the judgment brings, or else Karma would come to you too. This is why we so strongly encourage you to move away from judgment. This is how Karma can move much more swiftly. This is why Karma doesn't seem to come to specific individuals in the public eye or why it takes so long. There is too much judgment energy surrounding them. Life is benevolent in this way. It doesn't want to harm the wrong people.

May: Serenity
Time for a Reboot

1. You may not be considered very old in earth years, or you could be in your sixties, seventies, eighties, or even nineties, and yet the one thing

that everyone has in common is that their operating system is such an antique that it could be in the prehistoric man section of any of the great history museums. Yes, it has adapted to the times and yet it has done so without any change to its fundamental nature, which is "me first." The ego is this system that I refer to now and have so often spoken of. The main problem is that it only recognizes approximations of love, not the real thing. Real one hundred percent unconditional love cannot be recognized by the ego because there isn't any "me" in it. Unconditional love only has room for "we." Rebooting the ego with soul is long overdue. The fusion of the two, with the soul being superior, dominant, and recognized as such, is the only way to save humanity from itself. We need more constructive forces, not destructive ones. May this reboot be robust, widespread, and successful.

2. Week 1: What gives you a serene state of mind? Focus on the little things in life that bring you pleasure and serenity. List them and return to this list often to choose things off of it and enjoy them as often as possible.

3. Week 2: Do you have any relationships that give you serenity? Whether they are current relationships or ones from the past, revisit these characters this week and know that their souls were strong enough to bring the wonderful gift of serenity to both of you. Write about these relationships.

4. Week 3: The best way to experience serenity, or peace of mind, is to be in the Holy Instant as often and as long as possible. Write about your experiences with the Holy Instant this week.

5. Week 4: This week, write about a time, even for a fleeting moment, when you felt a sense of serenity during times of personal turmoil. Even though your mind was telling you otherwise, your soul was saying that everything was going to be okay.

6. Remaining Days of the Month: Why is serenity important in such a chaotic world? Explore this topic in your writing this week.

7. Imagine a place inhabited by humans who are only concerned for the well-being of others, including themselves, without being in opposition to others. Cooperation instead of competition will be the new mantra for everyone. This is what a reboot from fear to love, from ego to soul, will provide for you personally and for all who will allow it. Souls are coming into their own "I Am" power and are ready for this gargantuan challenge. They have waited patiently, as long as humans have been on the earth. Remember, soul power equals God power. How can things here not change when God is in charge?

June: Peace
The Ego Was the First Version of Artificial Intelligence

1. Everyone is talking about AI (artificial intelligence) and how useful and potentially destructive it is and could be, but the truth about AI is that it was created by and is being developed by artificial intelligence, which is the human ego. Yes, AI created AI. The human ego is artificial intelligence because it is not connected to universal intelligence or reality. It is this self-centered system that has its own identities, its own thoughts, its own purposes, its own reasoning and justification, its own belief systems, and its own perceptions (judgments). None of these things are based in truth or reality. They are based on an artificial reality, which is the human experience. Artificial intelligence that stems from computers that are programmed by humans is actually AI 2.0. It is one more step away from reality, which is now a total of two steps away from it.

2. Week 1: How does peace show up in your life experience? If you have peace because you go out of your way to avoid conflict, then is it truly

peace or just a stalemate, a temporary ceasefire? Explore this prompt this week in your journal writings.

3. Week 2: This week, take a close look at your family relationships. Which relationships have always been peaceful? Which of these feature regular communication (phone, text, email, social media, or in person)?

4. Week 3: Returning to Week 2, which family relationships have had periods where there has been a lack of peace, due to conflict of some type? What was it that helped remedy the situation(s)? Which relationship did this only happen once in and which relationship has it happened more than once? Which relationship had conflict so severe that it severed the bond?

5. Week 4: Now that you live a soul-based lifestyle, you realize that I'm telling you something that you are already well aware of, which is that you are in relationship mostly with ego-dominant individuals. You are likely now insisting that these relationships be as peaceful and authentic as possible. This week, write about the challenge this presents to you.

6. Remaining Days of the Month: Have you left relationships because you find that they are too draining on your deeply held commitment to and insistence on peace? Explore this topic in your journal writings this week.

7. Here's a question for you. Should humans fear AI? The answer is an emphatic yes. It was made by human AI, whose operating system is infused with fear, and fear only makes more of itself. Human governments already know about the frightening possibilities with AI and are drafting legislation to control it. Here's another question for you. What is control? Do you remember? It is part and parcel with fear. It is a product of it. Over time, humans will devise more and more laws restricting the use of AI, but it will grow to be more menacing, nonetheless. It will be a menace as humans have been a menace. The soul isn't afraid of anything. It only observes what is. While the soul grows in individuals and in

society at large, all things that are ego based, including AI, will be seen for what they are. Interest will wane because the truly exciting creation with unlimited growth potential is the soul, not a computer.

July: Enjoyment
I Can't Do This Alone; You Have Work to Do

1. Besides the fact that my teachings were so distorted or strangely missing entirely, the made-up stories that replaced the truth were truly unbelievable. Supposedly, if your average run-of-the-mill Jack or Jill simply believed that I lived on after I was killed, then they would be magically rewarded when I came out of the sky to usher in one thousand years of peace, while miraculously solving every believer's individual and collective problems. No, sorry to be the one who tells you this, but it doesn't work that way. Nothing works that way. Practicing Christ Consciousness takes dedication, discipline, and frankly, some very hard work that only you can do. If you have a perceived problem, then only you can solve it, with the guidance of your soul of course. That is your job while you are here on the magnificent earth canvas; solve all of your problems with love, instead of fear as your guide. It's that simple and that hard and I absolutely can't do it for you. My job is and always has been to simply point you in the right direction. The rest is up to you, my friends.

2. Week 1: This week explore all of the things that you enjoy. Does being soul driven change any of these experiences for you? If so, explain how in your journal writings.

3. Week 2: Reflect back to a time period where you were very much ego

driven. Describe your passions from this time period. Do you feel the same way about them now that you are soul driven? If so, explain how in your journal writings this week.

4. Week 3: This week, I want you to make a list of everything you enjoy experiencing. Then, I want you to promise yourself that you will do everything in your power to do these things as often as your heart desires.

5. Week 4: Reflect on your relationships this week. Understand that those you are in relationship with may have listed spending time with you in their list from Week 3. Throw withholding out the window and let yourself be seen and heard by those who love and care about you.

6. Remaining Days of the Month: Remember this! I am asking you (firmly) to prioritize enjoyment in your life experience. Quality enjoyment at the soul level is one of the best experiences you can have here. Live it up (responsibly). Your soul will thank you.

7. I hope by now you see that it would be quite impossible for me to save anyone since it's thoughts that cause problems for people individually and collectively and these thoughts are from the ego, which is creator of and part of the illusionary world. Only you can save yourself from yourself by opening up and listening to your soul instead of your ego, and as I've so often said, this is not an easy thing to do. The ego does not want to be put on the back burner, so it may like the idea of its host watching me come out of the sky without doing the work necessary to move it out of the way. The ego does not want to lose its power that it has held since the very start of the earth project. Sadly, everyone here has been deeply deceived by the ego, and the savior narrative is only one of the many, many deceptions.

August: Solitude
Now the Real Fun Begins

1. Now that you know the truth about the upside down, inside out world that you live in, navigating it as a soul-based character will at least be somewhat easier. You will understand why you see the things that you do in the world. They may still be heartbreaking and hard to look at, but you will have hope now that all have a magnificent opportunity that they have never had before, which is to be educated with a real education that is easily accessible to all. This education will replace millions of years of miseducation and will lay everything out in the open for all who are willing to see. They will discover who they are in truth and who I Am in truth. They will see that I Am just like them and not special in any way, shape, or form. Recreating the human world is to start over from a place of truth, not illusionary lies. *Soul in the Driver's Seat* is my love letter to humanity, a course where all is laid bare for all to see, a giant reset button, a second chance, a second coming of sanity when all can have fun recreating absolutely everything.

2. Week 1: Are you afraid of being by yourself or are you comfortable with it? Explore this topic this week. Why would someone need constant companionship from other people, pets, or noise from media? What purpose would this serve? Do you fall in this category?

3. Week 2: If you aren't someone who enjoys being by themselves, let me ask you this, have you tried it? Other people, especially ego-driven characters, are often time- and peace-consuming. This week, there is no suggested writing prompt. There is just a suggestion. Try being by

yourself at times during this week. No media. No background noise. Just you.

4. Week 3: This week, let this be your mantra, I don't need anyone or anything to fulfill me. I am enough. I don't need my phone, a computer laptop or desktop or tablet, a television screen, background chatter, or music. If I partake in these things, it is because I want to, not because I have to.

5. Week 4: Are you a conversationalist? If so, let solitude infuse your in-person, screen, or phone sharing. Instead of feeling like you need to fill in all of the spaces in a conversation, just let them be what they are, just pauses. Solitude lives in pauses. Write about a recent conversation. Was solitude part of it?

6. Remaining Days of the Month: One of the best places to be in solitude is outside. If the weather isn't conducive to spending time outside where you live, due to the season, the solution is an easy one. Picture yourself at your favorite outdoor location through journaling.

7. Now you can put aside all have-tos and supposed-tos. These come from the ego and the soul doesn't subscribe to them at all. It does things based on its own timing and its own ways of doing things. It does things because it wants to. It doesn't need a reason. A soul could want to celebrate Christmas on April 17, with a tree and presents for all. Characters need reasons and souls don't. They are free to have restriction-free fun, giving love anywhere and everywhere. The ego always wants to put brakes on "crazy" ideas, but by now, surely your brakes are completely worn out. Instead of replacing them, let your soul drive you at one hundred miles per hour without breaks. No one will get hurt, and you will have the time of your life. For once, you will start living a life of true freedom, and once you taste freedom you won't want to go back to stop-and-go traffic.

September: Togetherness
Being a Creator Is Messy Work

1. Besides getting rid of your brakes, here are more things to discard. You can throw away the following things: happy endings, periods at the end of sentences, tidy situations where everything neatly fits into perfectly sized boxes, pleasantries, and rigid role-playing. Instead, bring these things into your life: things that you don't understand, things you've never tried before, things that don't make sense, things you don't need but need you, unrealistic things, and anything wildly spectacular. Give yourself permission to be messy as you extend love to yourself and others. Throw away the rule book and be the person you were always meant to be. See where your soul, in conjunction with life, wants to take you. Let yourself be surprised and surprising around every turn in your brakeless car.

2. Week 1: What kind of people do you like spending time with? How would you describe your interactions; are they more ego-based or is their soul there too? This week, explore your current relationships in your journal. How can you infuse more soul into these relationships?

3. Week 2: Are you involved in any relationships that have run their course? Are you holding on to something that does not serve you any longer? Why? What are you afraid might happen if you break free? Explore this topic in your journal this week.

4. Week 3: Typically, soul-based individuals are not sought out as friendship material because people don't know what to make of them. There can't be a user/usee for an ego-soul friendship. An ego may call you when the chips are down, but they won't seek you out ordinarily.

How will you handle change or even loss in relationships with ego-based individuals?

5. Week 4: Unfortunately, I have to say this, but the world's relationships are a cesspool by and large. Soul-based relationships are beautiful spring waters in comparison. How can you begin or strengthen bonds with other soul-based individuals in the world? This is the definition of togetherness.

6. Remaining Days of the Month: As a strong soul of God, you will bless everyone near and far. This is your new relationship status. You are the sun, and all other creatures can bask in your powerful light, strengthening their souls in the process.

7. Remember this please. You are creating love by being a new you, shedding things connected to the old identity that kept you from your power source. This is usually a slow process. You will shed or discard when you are good and ready to do so, when you have withdrawn value from them. The more soul that you have driving your brakeless car, the freer you will feel and be. The freer you are, the less bound up you feel, the more creative you will be. What will you create? More soul in not only you but everyone surrounding you. Heat energy spreads. The closer someone is to you, the more heat they will receive. What is this heat energy? It's unconditional love. It's soul. It's God. More god equals increased influence in a single form or life and the collective. Now, let's answer one last question about being a creator. Do you ask for or wish for specific things for an individual or group of individuals? No. It already knows what to do. It paints the painting that it wants to paint, all by itself. Once this energy is extended from you, it takes on a life of its own as it joins with the soul that has always been there. This is simply known as blessing. It is the secret of the universe. This page has the secret of the universe written on it. Put a star on this page and return to it often, please.

October: Wholeness
Divine and Mortal

1. You are now a divinely mortal being. You are an individualized combination of the old and the new. You will or already have gotten rid of some of the old and allowed the soul to replace what had formerly been in that space (the ego). You will not entirely get rid of the ego. You need it here. Without it, no one would recognize you because your personality, your ways of being, would not be there anymore. Believe it or not, you will keep these parts of your ego even after you leave your earth experience. If you don't believe me, read parts of *A Journey into the Unknown* that features people in the public eye who have crossed over into the spirit realm. They have new perspectives in most, but not all cases, and they are still recognizable to those who knew them or knew of them. Even I have shreds of the old that I have kept so others will still recognize me. No one would recognize pure light energy. It is generic. This is another page you should star.

2. Week 1: The ego promotes fractured parts that fail to work together in a unified way. The soul, on the other hand, promotes unity within and without. This week, instead of writing about this or that, write about the whole, unified you, held strongly together by your soul.

3. Week 2: Now, expand on last week's topic and write about how your soul unifies you with the external world.

4. Week 3: This week, write about wholeness between your soul, or you as soul, and all of creation (God).

5. Week 4: Knowing that ideas such as good and bad belong to the ego, this week, reframe these ideas that you used to have about parts of you,

and see them through the lens of the soul, through wholeness.

6. Remaining Days of the Month: Wholeness is the healed you. Write about what things have healed through acceptance in the embrace of love.

7. Look around you. With a rare exception here and there, no one you see thinks of themselves as divine. Mortal, yes, but divine no. Everyone here is both, but due to the complete absence of education about the soul, as well as the distorted lies found in man-made religion, they think that divinity does not include them. They may think that God is divine. Angels are divine. I AM divine, but not them. They are just lowly, fallible humans. Hopefully, after receiving this very thorough, high-quality education about your soul and your ego, you no longer count yourself among the doubting Thomases. You know that you are both divine and mortal. This knowledge will only get stronger and will never leave you. I promise you this.

November: Kindness
Who Knew?

1. Who knew that there is something true here, something that very few know of? It is so well hidden in plain sight. The ego does not want anyone to see it, and for a very long time the soul was okay with the status quo. It lived as a second-class citizen, prevented from expressing. Remember, this is God who is being prevented from expressing. Times have changed now, and the soul is taking over. God is taking over this great planet, one body at a time. Soon, all will know this truth that was right in front of them this whole time. Who knew?

2. Week 1: Let's celebrate kindness in all shapes and sizes this month,

but instead of focusing on all of the ways that you have shown kindness to yourself and others, let's just say that we know that this is true just to save precious time. This month, I want you to spend the entire month focusing on all the wonderful acts of kindness others have shown you. This week, start with your family.

3. Week 2: Now, move on to close friends you have had in this current lifetime.

4. Week 3: This week, focus on acts of kindness you have received from acquaintances throughout your current lifetime.

5. Week 4: Next, focus on coworkers in your workplaces as an adult.

6. Remaining Days of the Month: Finally, this week, please journal about random acts of kindness from complete strangers. If you are addressing this month's prompts in a thorough fashion, expect tears to stain these pages. It is easy to forget, but many, many people have blessed you in many wonderful ways, dear one.

7. This news is very good news. It's the type of news that seems unbelievable and wonderful at the same time. The news that there is something true about humanity, about life, is amazing. Once the soul is ready to start assuming control from the ego, the character will be led to the right educational material, so that wholeness can be restored, so that the journey toward truth can begin. It won't be easy for anyone to go through this process, but remember that famous saying that your grandparents probably told you. If it's worth doing, it's worth investing your time and doing it right. What is two years or four years for the most dedicated, out of an entire lifetime? Turning from a completely ego-driven character to a soul-dominant character will be a miracle for anyone, especially those who didn't even know about the soul to begin with. Now, the secret is out. Shout it from the rooftops; there is something true here. God is not dead, but is alive and well inside of you. Hallelujah.

December: Wisdom
Here's a New Pronoun: We

1. In today's world, a small group of people are not happy with the names their parents have given them or ideas society has about their bodies. So, in search of their true identities, those with the typical and traditional pronouns may change them to the opposite and then try to conform to those sets of ideas, or they may use "they/them" for both traditional, male/female genders or for neither one exclusively. Individuals in this group will insist that their wishes be conformed to, even by complete strangers or by people who have never even thought about the possibility of changing their names or pronouns, all in the pursuit of trying to find happiness within their identity. This drives many up the wall, while some try their best to be supportive. Psychologists go along to prevent suicides and have created ideas about how gender can be a separate set of feelings from a particular body and how typical or traditional people are now called cisgendered. All of this is novel and has been fueled by the advancements in medicine to allow people to go even further with these ideas with medications and surgeries. Now, many people have asked what Jesus would say about the transgender movement. I will, in turn, ask you, mature soul that you are, what do you make of this? The soul is a "we," not an individual exclusively. It is happy with its character's name and pronouns and would never inspire the character to change anything about themselves. It loves the character just as it is. No changes are required. The soul knows who it is (God). It is the ego who is always searching for identities and interestingly misses the true one.

2. Week 1: It is wise in this world to not give unsolicited advice. However, if you are asked and only if you are asked, realize that you are in a position now where you can share words of wisdom as a seasoned soul. What would you say about all of the many issues floating around in the ego world today? What would love or God say? Use more journal pages than usual this week.

3. Week 2: Shine light on situations currently going on in your family. What words of wisdom are your soul wanting to say through your journal writing?

4. Week 3: This week, shine light on situations currently going on with your group of friends and acquaintances. What does your soul want you to write this week?

5. Week 4: For the final week in the *Soul Companion* journal, shine a light on current and even old situations in your life experience. Especially take a look at things that were unwanted, confusing, and pain filled. What wisdom can your soul impart to give you any needed clarity about these?

6. Remaining days of the month: For these last few days, take a look at who you were through the eyes of love and who you have become, after completing all of this soul work. Congratulations are in order, dear one. You did it! You did the seemingly impossible. You became a wise soul. Bravo! My hat's off to you.

7. Any and all expressions of the me, myself, and I concepts are from the ego and its perceptions of separation. This is all they have been, all they are, and all they will be. The ego always asks the question, "who am I?" Then it fills in the blanks with thoughts and feelings that it doesn't understand. This has been going on since the beginning. The soul only cares about service to the oneself in the form of others. It is very much a collective, a we. Souls don't stand alone, and they are well aware of this fact. They don't care what their host characters

wear or look like. They just want them to move away from exclusive ego identification and toward soul identification. God is a we, not a me, myself, and I.

Chapter Four

Conclusion

1. It is with a heavy heart that I write these final words for a conclusion to *Soul Companion*. Whether you consciously realize it or not, I have been with you every step of the way, since page one of *Soul in the Driver's Seat: A Course in Miracles for Today*. For some of you, I have been with you much longer, as you have read my other major and less known works. *Soul in the Driver's Seat* is the book that I am the most pleased with because it truly gets my basic messages across in a plain and understandable way. This book will provide a deep education to readers about themselves, not just by me telling them things, but by having readers do some very heavy lifting and taking a hard look at their own thoughts, feelings, attitudes, and experiences. It wasn't easy to look at these things, was it? And it definitely wasn't easy to go even deeper by writing about them each week for two years. How did you approach *Soul Companion*? Did you complete the journal entries while doing the two years of experiences in *Volume One* of *Soul in the Driver's Seat*, or did you hold off on the journaling until you completed the two years of mirror exercises, in *Volume Three*, for maintenance? There is no right or wrong way when you follow your heart. Is this goodbye? There is no such thing, silly. I Am you and you are me in unity. This is the new way moving forward. Say goodbye to separation and hello to union with all, as the magnificent and divine OneSelf. If you want to read my other books, your soul will help you to find and access them, but you don't

need any more of the written word because you have become it. The truth now lives inside and as you.

2. Your brother in Christ, Jesus

Resources

Discover Soul
soul.cocreatingclarity.com/Discover

Discover Soul is a powerful online search facility enabling you to locate any phrase or word within your copy of the book, *Soul in the Driver's Seat: A Course in Miracles for Today*. What follows is a brief explanation of how to interpret the references offered in your search results.

There are four parts to *Soul in the Driver's Seat*, each part designated as follows:

Volume One	V1
Volume Two	V2
Volume Three	V3
Soul Companion	C

References to specific text within *Soul in the Driver's Seat* follow one of three patterns:

Part:Chapter.Paragraph

This is the pattern you'll find for the majority of this book.

An example – V1:2.11 refers to *Volume One*, Chapter Two ("The Basics"), paragraph 11.

It begins "*You are not the thing that looks back at you in the mirror.*"

Part:Chapter.MonthNumber.Paragraph

This is the pattern you'll find in the chapters that offer daily reflections for each month of the year. For these chapters, there is an additional number that denotes the month by calendar number. An example – V3:3.7.1 refers to *Volume Three*, Chapter Three ("Mirror Exercises"), July, paragraph 1.

It begins *"This month, focus on enjoyment."*

Part:Chapter.Introduction/Epilogue/Conclusion.Paragraph
This is a third pattern you'll encounter only rarely when you'll find the chapter number replaced by a letter – an Introduction is denoted by "I", an Epilogue by "E", and a Conclusion by "C".

An example – C:2.C.1 refers to *Soul Companion*, Chapter Two, Conclusion, paragraph 1.

It begins *"This was a deeper dive into the twelve ..."*

Soul Bytes Podcast

You'll find the *Soul Bytes Podcast* on the *CoCreating Clarity YouTube Channel*. Listen to friendly conversations that dive into the essential messages of *Soul in the Driver's Seat*. These conversations, AI generated from each chapter of the book, offer you the key messages of *Soul in the Driver's Seat*, in ten- to fifteen-minute bite-size pieces.

Soul in the Driver's Seat Website

Read *Soul in the Driver's Seat, Volume One* online at the Soul website **soul.cocreatingclarity.com**

Indra's Net of Jewels

Enjoy updates and insights relating to *Soul in the Driver's Seat* at **cocreatingclarity.com/indrasnet**

Related Works

A Journey into the Unknown
Received by Richard Curtis Greathouse

A Journey into the Unknown, received February 2020 to October 2021, consists of sixteen distinct parts. Jesus introduced *Journey* as the third and final book completing his *"seminal trilogy"* which began with *A Course in Miracles* (received by Helen Schucman in 1965) and continued with *A Course of Love* (received by Mari Perron in 1998). The purpose of *Journey* is to shepherd all open and willing hearts from Christ Awareness (*A Course in Miracles*) and Christ Consciousness (*A Course of Love*) deeply and fully into Christ Manifestation and to support them in this transformation. All sixteen parts of *Journey* are available at **JourneyHub.CoCreatingClarity.org**

Arrival
Received by Richard Curtis Greathouse

Arrival, received October 2021 to December 2025, comprises seven distinct series of messages. All the messages of *Arrival* offer practical support for willing hearts devoted to walking the world as Love in Form, as Christs. Each Arrival series deepens and strengthens the capacity to BE example lives each day, loving unconditionally and blessing all indiscriminately. All seven series of *Arrival* are available at **Arrival.CoCreatingClarity.org**

A Course of Love
Received by Mari Perron

Learn about *A Course of Love* at **acourseoflove.org**

Explore Mari Perron's work at **mariperron.com**

A Course in Miracles
Received by Helen Schucman
Learn about *A Course in Miracles: Original Edition* at **jcim.net**
Explore more related works at
jcim.net/acim-comparison-of-versions

Acknowledgements

From Rick Greathouse —

First and foremost, thank you to Christina Strutt and her CoCreating Clarity team. *Soul in the Driver's Seat* would not be available to anyone without them. Their hard work has enhanced and revealed the clarity and magic of the message this book offers to all willing hearts. Christina saw the immense potential of *Soul* and took it from there, and for that I am extremely grateful.

And gratitude to all the people who have played starring roles in my life experience: Ian, Hank, Lori; my parents, Lynn and Carl; my sister, Toni; my brother-in-law, David; my brothers, Brian and Eric; my great-grandmothers, Beula and Cora; my maternal grandparents, Eula and Curt; and my paternal grandparents, Opal and Chester.

From Christina Strutt —

With boundless gratitude to the CoCreating Clarity team.

To Rick, your trust in the clarity that came through me and your unwavering confidence in my ability to shape and offer your gifts to the world have made this book possible.

To my precious husband of fifty years, Colin, who stepped forward to transcribe *Soul Volumes One, Two, and Three* when I could not. Who created the *Soul* website, publishing a new installment of *Soul* every month from August 2023 through December 2025. Who created the powerful *Discover Soul* search facility for referencing both website and book. And who remains my staunchest supporter in bringing *Soul* out into the world. He shows me each day that the alchemy of *Soul in the Driver's Seat* is Real.

To my steadfast CoCreatrix and friend, Jo Nagle, a talented digital storyteller who designed *Soul's* vibrant book cover, who keeps me on track with *Soul Journey* newsletters and the *Soul Bytes* podcast, whose skills and expertise in Online Presence and Multimedia never cease to amaze me, and whose wide-open heart demonstrates the power of unconditional love in the business world.

To my trusty editor and dear friend, Lee Reznicek, who willingly transcribed *Soul Companion* from Rick's handwritten words, who copyedited and proofread the complete *Soul* manuscript, and whose deep knowing of my heart and soul held me steady through the most challenging moments of this project.

To my maternal grandfather, Joseph Thambiah Richards, whose love of metaphysical principles and legacy of land purchased in Malaya over a hundred years ago, seeded this book into being.

And our publishing team who has magically shepherded *Soul* from finished manuscript into this beautiful print book in just three months! Thank you for moving us all a huge step forward towards Jesus' goal that his message reach "every man, woman, and child" at this pivotal time.

Receiver Bio

Richard Curtis Greathouse is a devoted son, husband, father, brother, and friend. He is also an experienced teacher with thirty-one years in special and general education at the elementary, middle, and high school levels. During a twelve-year break from teaching, he was a civilian employee of the San Francisco Police Department, a job coach for adults with intellectual disabilities, and a community ambassador serving San Francisco's unhoused community in the South of Market business district, before returning to teaching again. Since February 2020, to his astonishment, he has found himself serving as receiver of several books from the unseen world, all of which he has generously and freely shared online. He lives in the city with his amazing partner, Hank. Together they love listening to music, going to concerts, reading, taking walks, and just hanging out. The one accomplishment he is proudest of is his role in birthing *Soul in the Driver's Seat: A Course in Miracles for Today* – a book he knows deep in his soul, will be a powerful gift to all who discover it.

Notes:

Notes:

Notes:

Notes: